Praise f
HOW SWEET T...

D0192149

In our world obsessed with change, this book helps us engage and anchor in the never-ending song to our King of kings. Hymns are the heart's cry of God's people for generations. Laura L. Smith helps them become new songs we sing to the Lord.

> —ANDI ROZIER, Vertical Worship

I love how Laura L. Smith reminds the reader why we should continue to make room for the rich theology and powerfully poetic language of the hymns of the past.

> —NICOLE HICKMAN, Drummer for Christian band
> I AM THEY

In a time when it seems easier than ever to find what divides us rather than what brings us together, this book is so important. Laura L. Smith reminds us that hymns connect us to the past and unite us in the present. When we sing these songs, our souls feel that sense of unity— both to those who have come before us and also to our brothers and sisters who sing beside us.

> —THE BUNDYS, who appeared on *The Voice*

There are few sweeter moments than hearing the voices of multiple generations singing together. Hymns do that. They unite. Their cadence and lyrical depth have been instrumental in my journey of worshiping in Spirit and truth. *How Sweet the Sound* reminds Jesus followers of their powerful impact.

> —HOLLY STARR, Christian recording artist

How SWEET *the* SOUND

The Power *and* Promise *of* 30 Beloved Hymns

LAURA L. SMITH

Our Daily Bread Publishing™

How Sweet the Sound: The Power and Promise of 30 Beloved Hymns
© 2020 by Laura L. Smith

All rights reserved.

Requests for permission to quote from this book should be directed to: Permissions Department, Our Daily Bread Publishing, PO Box 3566, Grand Rapids, MI 49501, or contact us by email at permissionsdept@odb.org.

Scripture quotations, unless otherwise indicated, are taken from the Holy Bible, New International Version®, NIV®. Copyright © 1973, 1978, 1984, 2011 by Biblica Inc.™ Used by permission of Zondervan. All rights reserved worldwide. www.zondervan.com.

Scripture quotations marked ESV are taken from the ESV® Bible (The Holy Bible, English Standard Version®), copyright © 2001 by Crossway, a publishing ministry of Good News Publishers. Used by permission. All rights reserved.

Scripture quotations marked KJV are taken from the Authorized Version, or King James Version, of the Bible.

Scripture quotations marked MSG are taken from *The Message*, copyright © 1993, 2002, 2018 by Eugene H. Peterson. Used by permission of NavPress. All rights reserved. Represented by Tyndale House Publishers, a Division of Tyndale House Ministries.

Scripture quotations marked NLT are taken from the Holy Bible, New Living Translation, copyright © 1996, 2004, 2015 by Tyndale House Foundation. Used by permission of Tyndale House Publishers, Inc., Carol Stream, Illinois 60188. All rights reserved.

Scripture quotations marked TPT are from The Passion Translation®. Copyright © 2017, 2018 by Passion & Fire Ministries, Inc. Used by permission. All right reserved. ThePassionTranslation.com.

Library of Congress Cataloging-in-Publication Data

Names: Smith, Laura L., 1969- author.
Title: How sweet the sound : the power and promise of 30 beloved hymns / Laura L. Smith.
Description: Grand Rapids, MI : Our Daily Bread Publishing, 2020. | Summary: "Showcases 30 popular hymns and explores the timeless truths and emotions expressed by the hymn writers"-- Provided by publisher.
Identifiers: LCCN 2020011099 | ISBN 9781640700505 (paperback)
Subjects: LCSH: Hymns--Devotional use. | Hymns--History and criticism.
Classification: LCC BV340 .S65 2020 | DDC 264/.23--dc23
LC record available at https://lccn.loc.gov/2020011099

ISBN: 978-1-64070-050-5

Interior design by Beth Shagene

Printed in the United States of America

21 22 23 24 25 26 27 / 8 7 6 5 4 3 2

To sweet Jesus who saved a wretch like me.
I have no songs to sing without you,
and there's no place I'd rather be than in the middle
of your amazing grace.

To my incredible husband, Brett,
who shows me daily what Christ's love looks like.
I am better and stronger and happier
because of you in my life.
I will be madly in love with your amazing self
until all the songs have been sung.

CONTENTS

Introduction

HOW CAN A HYMN DO THAT?

My son plays electric guitar in the worship band at our contemporary church. Recently, they played "All Hail King Jesus" by Bethel Music. At the end of this particular song, my son plucked out the refrain of the classic hymn, "Crown Him with Many Crowns." He'd heard someone else play it this way and liked how it sounded. It fit. Because Jesus is King of kings, so of course He should be crowned with many crowns (see Revelation 19:12).

As my son broke into that old hymn on his guitar, something unexpected happened to me.

I'm going to be honest. "Crown Him with Many Crowns" isn't my favorite hymn, but I heard it repeatedly growing up. I'm pretty emotional about worship. Okay, I'm just pretty emotional. One friend describes me as a walking, talking emoji, which I fully take as a compliment. As I raised my hands and sang along—perhaps louder than the people around me would have preferred—I actually envisioned Jesus on His throne. And it took my breath away.

It no longer felt like I was in my modern church—the large industrial room filled with rows of chairs, floodlights, and screens projecting the lyrics. My mind flew back to the church where I grew up—red carpet, white pews, pale blue cushions and all. I was transported.

I was no longer standing next to my daughter in her jeans and flannel shirt, but next to my mom wearing her silky green Sunday dress and the dusty, floral scent of White Linen perfume. My mom always held the burgundy leather hymnal between us so I could see the words, and in this moment I could hear Mom singing, *"Hark! How the heav'nly anthem drowns all music but its own!"*

How can just a few notes of a song move me like that?

Music has a powerful effect on the way we remember things—it can transport us back in time, vividly reminding us of sensory details. This is what happened to me. I heard the melody to "Crown Him with Many Crowns" and my internal time machine dialed up Central College Presbyterian Church in the suburbs of Columbus, Ohio, circa 1985. The silver pipes of the organ lined up in neat rows, the flowing robes of the choir, the wooden cross front and center. This experience wasn't a onetime wonder. This strong, powerful response from hearing a hymn has happened to me before. I hear a classic church melody and something deep inside me shifts. I have an almost subterranean experience; something buried far inside me weeps and worships at the sound of these timeless songs.

Has this happened to you?

For some of us raised in traditional churches, these particular songs of praise take us back to our childhood, and then further, and further. But no matter if these hymns are new or familiar, they can carry us back to the people who first wrote the words. Like us, these pilgrim poets loved God the Father, were filled with the Spirit, and clung fiercely to the salvation and hope of Jesus. There is life to be found in this music because it points us unabashedly toward Jesus. Because it proclaims the same hope and salvation we seek today.

Hymns have melodies written for organs, not electric guitars. They're nothing like the electronic music that's mastered and produced on computers with digital simulations of horns, drums, and strings that fills the charts and speakers of today. So what makes my seventeen-year-old decide to pick out these notes from the past and blare them through his amp? Why do modern Christian artists like Kristian Stanfill, Hillsong, Chris Tomlin, and Crowder incorporate hymns from over a hundred years ago into their repertoires?

I think it goes back to the lyrics my mom sang in my time warp: *Hark! How the heav'nly anthem drowns all music but its own!*

This is God's music—heavenly anthems written about our eternal, unchanging God. Lyrics often rooted in Scripture. The truths in these hymns, no matter when they were written, haven't changed. God is still good. The Lamb is still on His throne. He is still worthy. We still long to give Him endless praise.

The same largely holds true for the modern worship music I love. Tunes I belt out not only at church, but in my car, while I cook dinner, shower, and go on jogs.

Because modern worship music also points us to our King of kings. All songs written for our living, loving God can help us draw closer to Him.

Hymns from the past won't become outdated like vinyl records or cassette tapes. They are a special kind of music, packed with truth, redemption, and joy no matter how the times or culture change.

When we spend time immersing ourselves in these songs written to point us to Jesus, maybe, just maybe, these heavenly anthems will drown out the distractions of the world, will take us back, not just to our memories but to generations of people seeking Jesus. And maybe this music and these lyrics will inspire us to help modern generations become people who do the same—a twenty-first-century gathering of worshipers dedicated to pursuing Jesus in life and in song.

* * *

Note from the author: One criterion used in choosing the hymns for this book was that they must be in the public domain. This was done so I could share with you the lyrics to each hymn at the beginning of its coinciding chapter. The refrain or chorus for each hymn is included only once, although when playing or singing it might repeat between verses. You may be familiar with a different version of some of these hymns (such as "He Will Hold Me Fast" in chapter 23). Also, hymn lyrics are set in italics when quoted in or integrated into the text.

How
SWEET
the
SOUND

1

THE DOXOLOGY

Thomas Ken, 1674

Praise God, from whom all blessings flow;
Praise Him, all creatures here below;
Praise Him above, ye heavenly host;
Praise Father, Son, and Holy Ghost.

How Hymns Unite Us

Remember the last time you attended a concert? Can you recall the hum in the auditorium before the show started? The buzz as the sound system was tested and the snippets of conversations echoed in the concert hall? The energy as attendees scanned aisles and rows in search of seats, anticipating the show? The hush that came with the dimming of lights signaling something significant was about to start?

There's a unique atmosphere created by people coming together and anticipating something spectacular.

When my husband, Brett, received a text asking if we'd like to join friends to see the OUTCRY Tour, we were excited the show was nearby, our calendar was miraculously free, and the tickets were reasonably priced. When we saw the lineup—Vertical Worship, Mosaic MSC, Elevation Worship, Bethel Music, and Christine Caine—this event went from "fun idea" to "we will make this happen." We declined our friends' kind invitation for a double date and instead made it a Smith family outing.

We knew we were in for a night of worship, but we couldn't fully anticipate what to expect. Roadies placed guitars on stage. Mics were raised and lowered. One of our kids commented that they must be setting up all of the bands' instruments at once because it would take too much time to switch out sets between all the participating acts. That made sense to me. Moving around multiple drum kits, pedal boards, and so on would create a lot of dead time between four bands and a speaker.

But there was another reason all those instruments were precisely placed on stage before the first chord sounded. We just didn't know it yet.

The lights lowered and all of the built-up energy of the crowd surged. Thousands of people applauded the darkness because we knew it signaled the start of the show. It was as if a ringmaster had come out in red tails and top hat and announced, "Ladies and gentlemen, this is the moment you've been waiting for."

There was shuffling on stage. Musicians assembled. Wires were checked one final time . . . then *BAM!*

Praise God, from whom all blessings flow;
Praise Him, all creatures here below;
Praise Him above ye; heavenly host;
Praise Father, Son, and Holy Ghost.

Goosebumps.

"The Doxology," a simple hymn written more than three hundred years ago by a devout Anglican bishop. Thomas Ken intended it as the ending of the morning and evening songs he instructed his students at Winchester College to sing—not as the opening to an electrified concert.[1]

Yet even without lyrics projected on the screen, thousands of concert-goers, young and old—children and retired folk and every age in between—all sang along. It didn't matter if ticket-holders came from a traditional church, a house church, or a megachurch. It didn't matter if their church was liturgical, mainline, or evangelical. God's people knew the words. And we all joined in.

Everyone who entered that auditorium came with different needs and expectations. Some were hoping to see friends, others to hear inspirational teaching, and some to gain encouragement for their local church. Some longed for healing or a miracle, some came simply to see their favorite band. But no matter what divisions or differences we walked in with, we were all instantly united by just a few notes of a four-line hymn written in 1674—united by our voices lifted in praise to our God.

Cody Carnes, cocreator of OUTCRY, explains, "The enemy wants to tell us that we are alone. He wants us feeling disconnected and isolated. But nights like OUT-CRY help everyone see that we aren't on our own. We are all in this together. And that is a powerful thing."[2]

We're all different. During church services, some of us sit in wooden pews, some in comfy chairs. Some sit crisscross-applesauce on the floor, and some of us prefer to stand. Some of us believe this doctrine, others follow that one. There are multiple translations of the Bible, and different churches favor one over another. Some churches walk to the front for communion, others pass it around.

But some days, don't we get too tangled up in the details? In the differences? What if all of us "creatures here below" focused on praising God above everything else, above our personal habits and styles and traditions?

The apostle Paul said it like this in his letter to the Romans:

> May the God who gives endurance and encouragement give you the same attitude of mind toward each other that Christ Jesus had, so that with one mind and one voice you may glorify the God and Father of our Lord Jesus Christ. Accept one another, then, just as Christ accepted you, in order to bring praise to God. (Romans 15:5–7)

In that moment at the start of the OUTCRY Tour concert, when a simple doxology drew us all together in worship, I felt just a glimmer of what Paul so eloquently described: unity.

Hymns can do that.

A year ago I was invited to speak at a Women of the Word event in Indiana. I didn't know anybody in the area but eagerly agreed to speak because the venue was just half an hour away from where my daughter attended college. My secret plan was to teach three sessions, then sneak over to campus and take my little girl out to dinner.

The evening before the event, I entered the high school where the conference would take place for a sound check. I roamed the halls, passing the gym packed with spectators stomping their feet in excitement at a volleyball game and a wall decorated in student artwork—still-life pencil sketches of guitars and trumpets.

I eventually found some women setting up tables and was directed to Diane, who was in charge of the event. We hugged, and she introduced me to the women on the organizing committee. Then Diane suggested we all pray.

In a high school hallway, holding hands with women whom I'd met only moments before, Diane prayed the event would glorify God. The hand to my left was cool and crepe-like, lined with age and wisdom; the hand to my right, warm and young and strong. Diane prayed that women would come, that they would be spiritually fed, that the Holy Spirit would work in this place.

And then she broke into "the Doxology."

There was just an "Amen" and immediately after it, Diane's alto singing, "Praise God from whom all blessings flow." I don't know about the other ladies standing in our circle, but I didn't see it coming.

But it didn't matter. We all knew this song. "The Doxology" is an anthem of God's people. No matter where we've come from or what we're looking for. No matter what we're anticipating or dreading.

We come together. Praising God from whom everything good comes. All of us, all of His people here below, praising Him. Praising Him above anything else in our lives, anyone we consider important—thought leaders, pastors, even above angels. Praising God, three in one, Father, Son, and Holy Ghost.

CONTEMPLATE

Accept one another, then, just as Christ accepted you, in order to bring praise to God. (Romans 15:7)

1. When was a time you felt truly accepted by a group of Christian people (beyond the walls of your church)? Describe it.

2. Why do you suppose worshiping God is such a uniting force for us?

3. How can you apply the uniting message of "The Doxology" to somewhere you'll be this week? Maybe by inviting or including someone who might not feel comfortable or welcome?

2

PRAISE TO THE LORD, THE ALMIGHTY

Joachim Neander
Original German 1680
Translated by Catherine Winkworth in 1863

Praise to the Lord, the Almighty, the King of
creation!
O my soul, praise Him, for He is thy health and
salvation!
All ye who hear, now to His temple draw near,
Join me in glad adoration!

Praise to the Lord, who o'er all things so wondrously
reigneth,
Shelters thee under His wings, yea, so gently
sustaineth!
Hast thou not seen, how thy desires e'er have been
Granted in what He ordaineth?

Praise to the Lord, who hath fearfully, wondrously,
made thee;

Health hath vouchsafed and, when heedlessly falling,
    hath stayed thee.
What need or grief ever hath failed of relief?
Wings of His mercy did shade thee.

Praise to the Lord, who doth prosper thy work and
    defend thee;
Surely His goodness and mercy here daily attend thee.
Ponder anew what the Almighty can do,
If with His love He befriend thee.

Praise to the Lord, who, when tempests their warfare
    are waging,
Who, when the elements madly around thee are
    raging,
Biddeth them cease, turneth their fury to peace,
Whirlwinds and waters assuaging.

Praise to the Lord, who, when darkness of sin is
    abounding,
Who, when the godless do triumph, all virtue
    confounding,
Sheddeth His light, chaseth the horrors of night,
Saints with His mercy surrounding.

Praise to the Lord! O let all that is in me adore Him!
All that hath life and breath, come now with praises
    before Him!
Let the Amen sound from His people again,
Gladly for aye we adore Him!

How Hymns Fill Us with Gratitude

I have the most amazing group of women in my Bible study.

No, they're not superheroes, or "super-Christians." But they *are* loving, funny, and insightful—all beautiful in their own ways. They ask phenomenal questions and give incredible responses that encourage and challenge me. I sit and follow their thoughts like a ping pong match, my head pivoting back and forth trying to absorb it all.

One thing we like to do before we dig into the material we're studying is to go around and share something we're thankful for. It can be tricky to switch gears from the deadlines, data, and distractions ladies are focused on before entering the room. But somehow, coming up with something we're thankful for is simple—and it works. We don't have to have completed the homework or memorized a verse or thought too hard. We can find a reason to be thankful almost on demand. And speaking out loud something for which we are grateful mentally turns the page for us, at least it does for me—away from my planner and towards my Savior.

The responses are as varied as the women sitting in a circle on black plastic chairs in the church room where we meet.

One mom in her twenties has a son with cystic fibrosis. She shares that the doctor called saying the antibiotics for her son worked! The bacteria have cleared from his lungs.

A grandma comments on her beautiful drive coming to the church, the changing colors of the leaves, the fog lifting and allowing the sun to shine through.

An empty nester thanks God for her full garden and proceeds to pass out bags of crisp, green lettuce she's brought for each of us.

Someone is thankful for her kids, another her husband, one for a cozy sweater on a brisk fall morning, yet another for the Bible—that it exists for her to learn more about God. It's beautiful to hear all the gratitude. Not one woman had the same thing top-of-mind on her thankful list. And yet, we all nod because we are all grateful for healing, family, God's Word, His creation, warmth, and that Linda brought us fresh lettuce.

Even more incredible?

Not one woman is thankful for something she's done herself, that she has any control over. It's as if we're singing in the background of our discussion the old German hymn "Praise to the Lord, the Almighty." The wording of this hymn tripped me up as a kid. I sang the lyrics out loud week after week, but because they weren't written the way I spoke, I didn't pay attention to what any of them meant. But relistening after all these years, the lyrics ring so true.

All ye who hear, now to His temple draw near, join me in glad adoration!

All us Bible study ladies are drawing near to His temple (well to the youth room at the end of the kids' wing in our contemporary church, but same idea) and joining together in thankfulness.

The hymn talks about God's great love, about all that He provides for His people! God really is so good.

It's one thing when I think of all the things He's done and is doing in my life, but to look around the room and listen to all the incredible ways God is weaving His love into the lives of women around me magnifies my ability to see how great His love is. Without these women, I'd have a much narrower vision of God. Because of them, I get a panoramic view.

And each of my Bible study ladies, despite their various life stages, the large variances in how long and how they've been seeking God, despite their different socio-economic situations, each one knows that all the goodness comes from Jesus.

The young mom didn't cure her son's infection. Yes, she and her husband took their little guy to his specialist at the children's hospital for an appointment. Yes, they scraped together the money needed to purchase the expensive prescription. Yes, this mama administered antibiotics to a one-year-old day after day with a two-year-old running circles around them. Was it easy? No. Was she faithful? Yes. Did she cure him? No. Did God? Yes!

Did the woman in her seventies paint the leaves golden yellow and deep scarlet? Did she coerce the fog into swirling across the pavement and into the atmosphere? Of course not. Did she take time to breathe it in, to give credit to the Creator? To draw all of our attention to His artwork on this Tuesday morning? Yes. And I'm so grateful she did. But there's no arguing: all of the credit goes to God, *the King of creation*.

Sure, we married our spouses and birthed our babies, but no way could I take credit for my husband or kids. The other women seem to feel the same way.

The whole God-growing-four-different-tiny-people-inside-my-belly-over-the-years is mind-boggling! Plus, I personally dated "the wrong guy"—make that wrong *guys*—over and over again. The fact that I get to spend my life with my husband after I actively sought to spend time with all of those Mr. Wrongs is nothing short of a miracle. My husband listens to my rants, holds me when I cry, tells me I'm beautiful. These were all things I was seeking, yet I couldn't invent a guy that would be all of these things for me. Only God could do that. God loves and provides for messed-up, messy me. It's too much to get my mind around. He loves me despite my flaws, and somehow gets Brett to peek through His almighty lens when he looks my way. It makes me *ponder anew what the Almighty can do.*

And this may sound trivial—lettuce and a sweater—food and clothing, but hey, I think we're all wearing clothes today, right? (I mean if you're not, why don't you put the book down and go put something on? I'll wait.) And I'm guessing we probably all ate food today. But we couldn't without God. No matter how stylish we are or what fabulous cooks we are, no matter how often we post stunning pics of our outfits and meals on social media, no matter how much we drool over other people's recipes, none of it happens without God. Not a bit. Not a fresh herb takes root in the ground. Not a sheep grows wool that will be sheared and woven into that warm sweater. Not without God.

Hast thou not seen, how thy desires e'er have been, granted in what He ordaineth?

Yes, God provides all of our needs, not because He has to do this for us, but because He is so very gracious. Food, clothes, shelter—all of it comes from God.

And this is just a handful of thank-you notes to God in His giant mailbox, just a quick glance of what popped into a dozen ladies' minds in a room with an orange couch and teenage doodles on a whiteboard this specific morning. It also amazes me that not a single one of these women would have gathered here—despite the sugary Funfetti cookies and the freshly brewed coffee—if it weren't for Jesus dying on the cross for each of us.

Because yes, spectacular scenery and medicines that heal are glorious things. But there's something much more glorious. Each of the women in the room inspires me and I love chatting with them about everything from our favorite shows to the armor of God.

But I know each lady has a past.

A list of arguments she's been in, choices she's made, things she's tried or said, which she wishes she hadn't. I know, from listening to and praying with these women week after week that all of them have triggers, real-life struggles with self-image, relationships, and finances.

Despite the ways they don't have it all together, despite their many failings, Jesus looked at each one of them and communicated a message like this: "I love you so much. I know what I'm about to face is unbearable—the humiliation of all the words people are about to say about me. The pain of nails piercing my hands and feet. Not being able to catch a breath as my lungs collapse for you on the cross. But, of course, I'll do it. It's all worth it. Why? Because I love you. I love you so very much."

And that's where Jesus's mercy undoes me. It's one thing to be grateful for sweaters and snuggles from kiddos on fall mornings, but another to realize my life has been *changed* because of what He's done. Because Jesus gave up His life for me, for you, *His goodness and mercy* shall *daily attend* us.

What are you thankful for today? Can you honestly take credit for an ounce of it? Who gave you that skill set? That opportunity? That connection? That relationship? Who created the heart in your chest that's currently pumping blood through your body? Who loved you so much that He died for you, so you could stand here today, able to give thanks?

There are things about God I'll probably never understand, like how He can love us so immeasurably. How He can see to every detail of landscapes and heartbeats and conversations and snacks. And why He showers glorious gifts upon us on a daily basis, despite the things we've said and done to Him, and to His children.

God's love? So deep I cannot fathom it.

Praise to the Lord! O let all that is in me adore Him!

CONTEMPLATE

May I never boast except in the cross of our Lord Jesus Christ, through which the world has been crucified to me, and I to the world. (Galatians 6:14)

1. For what are you thankful today? Why?

2. When you "ponder anew what the Almighty can do," what comes to mind? What amazes you about what God does for you?

3. What's one thing you can do each day this week to give your own personal "Praise to the Lord, the Almighty"? Maybe start a gratitude journal listing things you're grateful for, or write a thank-you note telling someone you're thankful God put them in your life.

3

GO DOWN, MOSES!

Traditional African American spiritual,
Author Unknown

When Israel was in Egypt's land,
Let my people go,
Oppressed so hard they could not stand,
Let my people go.

> *Go down, Moses,*
> *Way down in Egypt's land,*
> *Tell old Pharaoh,*
> *Let my people go.*

The Lord told Moses what to do,
Let my people go,
To lead the Hebrew children through,
Let my people go.

The pillar of cloud shall clear the way,
Let my people go,
A fire by night, a shade by day,
Let my people go.

As Israel stood by the waterside,
Let my people go,
At God's command it did divide,
Let my people go.

When they had reached the other shore,
Let my people go,
They sang the song of triumph o'er,
Let my people go.

O, let us all from bondage flee,
Let my people go,
And let us all in Christ be free,
Let my people go.

How Hymns Free Us

If you walk far enough through downtown Cincinnati, Ohio, you'll eventually arrive at the National Underground Railroad Freedom Center.

Take a moment here to look around. The entire modern concrete-and-glass building is a tribute to those who were or are enslaved, and their fights for freedom. The exhibits range from original black-and-white sketches of the horrific slave ships that transported tens of thousands of Africans to America, to a modern documentary about Nelson Mandela flickering in a small theater.

You'll also find a heartbreaking multimedia art piece strewn with fuzzy carpet fibers depicting present-day child slavery in the carpet industry of India. Rough wooden signs on seemingly handmade street posts direct visitors to an interactive video that begins with an actor explaining how he wants to escape his plantation in the South during the Civil War. The "slave" describes a set of his circumstances, and then you must decide his next move.

Should he try to escape now, in the cold of winter?

Should he postpone and make his escape attempt when it's warmer?

Should he climb a tree and hide?

Or make a run for it?

When hunting dogs are barking down the trail behind him, should he cut open a pungent onion and rub it on the soles of his shoes?

Or trudge through the icy cold water?

After you make each choice, the actor comes back on screen explaining what happened—the likely outcomes of your life-or-death decisions. These are choices real people had to make, and real consequences they endured.

All of the exhibits at this museum depict people enslaved by crushing circumstances; people in bondage longing to break free. The entire atmosphere is solemn, contemplative. Lights are dim. Patrons speak in whispers, as if in a library. And "negro spirituals" are the soundtrack streaming softly from the speakers.

These hymns are a specific type of folk song, often attributed as early gospel, sung by slaves in the United States. Most slaves were prohibited from learning to read, but that didn't stop them from learning stories of faith and applying them to their lives. These spirituals were sung in praise houses during Sunday worship and out in the sweltering fields while picking prickly cotton blossoms. The most popular of these songs were ones that resonated with the horrific state of slaves' lives—being treated like property. Some of the more familiar to us today are "Swing Low, Sweet Chariot," or "Rock My Soul in the Bosom of Abraham."

And of course, "Go Down, Moses!"[1]

Songs about slavery and the Promised Land resonated with American slaves, just like certain hymns and modern songs resonate with us and the issues we face in our daily lives. But slaves also used some of these spirituals as passwords along the Underground Railroad, the system of secret routes that helped them escape to freedom in Canada. For example, Harriet Tubman was a freed slave who helped over seventy others find freedom. She sang "Go Down, Moses!" as code, identifying herself as someone who could be trusted to assist runaway slaves.[2]

But the power of "Go Down, Moses!" and the longing for escape weren't erased when slaves were emancipated.

Most of us can't imagine actual slavery, but some of us feel enslaved in other ways, don't we? Maybe we feel enslaved to a job, or a toxic relationship, or to shame from the past, or a number on the bathroom scale, or a mountain of debt, or to demands from others. We might suffer from depression or anxiety, and maybe some days even struggle to get out of bed.

It's okay. We all long for freedom of one sort or another. It's just in the DNA of how we were created.

We all seem to have our own set of shackles that impede us from living freely in Christ. We feel trapped. We longingly look at the metaphorical Red Seas or borders into Canada we'd love to cross—freedom, so visible, yet seemingly unattainable.

What do you need to be liberated from today? The apostle Paul proclaims this in his letter to the Galatians,

> It is for freedom that Christ has set us free. Stand firm, then, and do not let yourselves be burdened again by a yoke of slavery. (Galatians 5:1)

And yet, some of us hold the keys to our cages and are afraid to unlock them, maybe because severing that toxic relationship just seems too hard. Maybe because admitting our past would be embarrassing. Because quitting that job would be too risky.

We don't need to all go out and do insanely drastic things to achieve emancipation, but Jesus has given us permission to walk freely with Him. The question is, what do we do with that freedom? It might be as simple as not being available the next time that awful person calls, or refusing to buy the food or drink that consumes you on your next grocery run. Or it might be harder, like renegotiating times and unreasonable schedules with your boss, or finding a support group that can help you take the first steps to recovery and healing.

We all have different circumstances and different keys, but freedom in all these situations starts with the same Jesus.

The story of Scripture is that God longs for freedom for His people. They keep finding themselves stuck, and God keeps rescuing them—over and over again. Near the beginning of the Bible, God sends Moses to free the Israelites from slavery in Egypt. The histories of Israel's judges and kings show repeatedly God intervening to rescue his children. God even sent Jonah—against his will!—to give the despicable Ninevites a second chance.

And then our New Testament begins. God incarnates himself into a little baby, sending "his one and only son" into the world so that "whoever believes in him shall not perish but have eternal life" (John 3:16). And after defeating death itself, Jesus commissions His disciples to share this incredible Good News. One day the end will come, in the grand finale in Revelation: Christ himself returns to save His people once and for all.

Of course we still face daily obstacles to freedom. Circumstances hem us in, get us stuck, lock us up. But standing in the lobby of the National Underground Railroad Freedom Center, listening once again to rich, suffering voices singing "Go Down, Moses!" I think to myself that it's time for you and me to embrace the freedom that Jesus brings—spiritual, emotional, relational and more.

Jesus's offer of freedom has no strings attached.

There's no expiration date.

Do you feel trapped today, like you don't know which way to go? Do you worry that maybe there is no way left for you?

Listen to the chorus singing behind you, friend. These are people who once endured more than you or I can imagine. These are the voices that speak truth to us again, reaching out to our hearts from lifetimes gone by, encouraging us to remember the news—that surprising, wonderful, redeeming good news.

> *O, let us all from bondage flee,*
> *Let my people go,*
> *And let us all in Christ be free,*
> *Let my people go.*

CONTEMPLATE

It is for freedom that Christ has set us free.
(Galatians 5:1)

1. What makes you feel trapped or caged in? When you feel this way, what do you do?

2. How does it make you feel to know that Christ wants to save you from the places where you feel stuck? Describe it.

3. The lyrics of "Go Down, Moses!" declare: "let us all in Christ be free." What does it mean to take Jesus up on that beautiful offer? Write out a prayer asking Him to help you do just that.

4

PSALM 96

Attributed to King David

Oh sing to the Lord a new song; sing to the Lord,
    all the earth!
Sing to the Lord, bless his name; tell of his
    salvation from day to day.
Declare his glory among the nations, his marvelous
    works among all the peoples!
For great is the Lord, and greatly to be praised; he
    is to be feared above all gods.
For all the gods of the peoples are worthless idols,
    but the Lord made the heavens.
Splendor and majesty are before him; strength and
    beauty are in his sanctuary.

Ascribe to the Lord, O families of the peoples,
    ascribe to the Lord glory and strength!
Ascribe to the Lord the glory due his name; bring
    an offering, and come into his courts!
Worship the Lord in the splendor of holiness;
    tremble before him, all the earth!

Say among the nations, "The LORD reigns! Yes, the
world is established; it shall never be moved; he
will judge the peoples with equity."
Let the heavens be glad, and let the earth rejoice;
let the sea roar, and all that fills it; let the field
exult, and everything in it!
Then shall all the trees of the forest sing for joy
before the LORD, for he comes, for he comes to
judge the earth.
He will judge the world in righteousness, and the
peoples in his faithfulness. (ESV)

How Hymns Point Us Back to What Matters

Instead of cranking up the volume to the music, which
normally helped propel me forward on my runs, I tuned
out the humming in my ears so I could mentally replay
the confrontation over and over again.

What if I had bit my tongue?

But I hadn't.

My pulse raced even though I'd started at a slow,
methodical pace and hadn't yet run a mile. *Ugh*. I longed
to connect with my son, not create walls between us.
Yet another part of me wanted to shake him after our
interchange. The bitter taste of anger still lingered on my
tongue as my feet rhythmically pounded the asphalt this
sticky July morning. I hated feeling this way.

As I passed a patch of deep purple petunias, the chorus of a familiar song in my earbuds faded to soft chords on a keyboard accompanied by a deep British accent.

Sing to the Lord a new song. Sing to the Lord all the earth.[1]

I turned up the volume. The abruptness of the change from upbeat tunes to deliberate words caught my attention, much like the immediate relief I experienced heading outside from the tension at home. Shade from giant oaks and maples standing like canopies over the manicured lawns brought relief from the beating sun. The thick, sweet scent of honeysuckle filled my senses as my mind shifted from the conversation I needed to have when I returned home to the immediacy of what played in my ears. The voice continued, *Sing to the Lord and bless His Name. Tell of His salvation from day to day.*

My feet stopped running.

I'd asked my son to do something hard. Something I knew he didn't want to do. I'd looked directly in his eyes. He saw me. He heard me. But he wished he hadn't. And as a defense mechanism against the thing he wished he hadn't heard, he turned, ignored me and my request, and stomped up the stairs, feet echoing like a snare drum. It was disrespectful. And my pride swept over me like a smoky purple cloud. The calm tone I'd been striving to maintain morphed into a villainous bark.

"Don't you walk away from me!"

I immediately recognized how worthless the words were. Somewhere in my past I could hear my mom shouting this same phrase to my brother. I could see in my memory him tromping up the green shag carpeted steps. And I could almost hear her audible sigh.

I called to my son.

Upstairs his door shut with a click.

We both needed time and space.

That's when I'd headed out for a run.

My feet and legs moved on autopilot while my soul pondered and prayed how to apologize for losing my temper. Sweat dripped from my eyebrows and down the sides of my face as I wondered how to emphasize the importance of this thing I'd asked my boy to do. My mind spun through multiple scenarios of what I should say, like retakes of movie scenes. Why was parenting so hard?

But now, I found myself standing, just standing in front of a stranger's house in a neighborhood where I don't live. My body couldn't dismiss the lyrics of the hymn I wasn't expecting to have proclaimed in my ears, couldn't just keep going on as if nothing had changed.

Because something had changed.

My cluttered thoughts vanished and were replaced by gratitude and awareness of what truly mattered. The beauty of the words and the power of our God, and yes, my deep down instinctual desire to praise Him overwhelmed me. Tears formed in the corners of my eyes. *Yes!* I thought. *Bless His name. Sing to the Lord!*

The voice in my earbuds, Andi Rozier of Vertical Worship, continued to recite Psalm 96.

For all the gods of the peoples are worthless idols,
But the Lord made the heavens.
Splendor and majesty are before Him.

Why was I so tangled and tense about a single conversation, when the Lord made everything, is in control of all the things, is almighty?

My "perfect mom" goals are worthless idols, not that they're unimportant, they're just not what should define me or my life with Jesus. I should love my kids to the best of my ability—but the details of one argument aren't worth freaking out about—they're like cars zipping by, noisy distractions.

Because God is great; He slices through the yuck pointing us back to what's truly important. I heard God whisper to me, *Listen. Look around.*

I pushed "stop" on my concerns and pushed "play" on the scene around me. Twittering birds. The hum of an airplane.

Let the field exult, and everything in it!
Then shall all the trees of the forest sing for joy.

Bright blooms, legs that can run, and a body God programmed to sweat to regulate its own temperature. Splendor and majesty are everywhere because God made it so. Glory is in His sanctuary! Not just in giant cathedrals and high mountaintops, but in sleepy neighborhoods where newspapers wait on driveways, and the dew has not yet burned off the grass.

The last word of Psalm 96 is "faithfulness."

God is faithful in every season. When we have infants who keep us up all night, teenagers who challenge us, or adult children with a new set of struggles. When we're single, married, divorced, or widowed, God is there. God is faithful both when we're constantly pushing "play" in our lives, and when we feel like our "stop" button is stuck in place. God is faithful when we're surrounded, and when we're alone. Because God *is* what fills us. He *is* who sustains us. Day after day. Year after year. He continues to give us new songs to sing.

This hymn is a stunning reminder of this truth. Every tree and fish sings praises to God—not because of their bank accounts, how many followers they have, or how they handled a certain interaction with another tree or fish, but because God created them, because He created the soil and sea for them to thrive in, because God is good. Because God is faithful.

This song, written we surmise by the ancient King David, a royal, Middle Eastern man who lived more than three thousand years ago, pulls this suburban middle-aged mama away from my modern problems and points me back to the Lord who created it all. This hymn transcends time, nationality, social status, and gender because it directs us to the thing that matters most—our God who created all of us from King David to me to you.

Psalm 96 is a hymn older than I can get my mind around, but it's also the inspiration for loads of additional hymns found in today's hymnals. I searched Hymnary.org for songs based on Psalm 96 and got 217 hits![2]

What's on your worry list today? What are your aches and issues? No matter our status we can, as the hymn instructs, *Worship the Lord*. We can *tremble* in awe and reverence of Him because look at what He has made— berries, biology, biceps, and bees that have wings that flap more than 230 beats per second[3]—that's quite a drum solo.

Look. Listen. I'm pretty sure there's something unbelievable within arm's reach—the juiciness of fresh watermelon, the miracle of rain falling from the sky to water the earth, the wet nose of your dog as he nuzzles your hand, or a song that points you back to the Creator. *Sing to the Lord. Bless His name.*

Hold on to that.

Run with it.

CONTEMPLATE

Sing to the LORD, all the earth. Sing to the LORD, bless his name. (Psalm 96:1–2 ESV)

1. What distractions and worries fill your head today?

2. Take a moment to look around you. What do you hear? What do you notice? What do you feel? Make a list of the incredible things around you. Praise God for them!

5

COME, THOU FOUNT OF EVERY BLESSING

Robert Robinson, 1758,
written for Pentecost

Come, thou fount of every blessing,
Tune my heart to sing thy grace;
Streams of mercy, never ceasing,
Call for songs of loudest praise.
Teach me some melodious sonnet,
Sung by flaming tongues above.
Praise the mount! I'm fixed upon it,
Mount of thy redeeming love.

Sorrowing I shall be in spirit,
Till released from flesh and sin,
Yet from what I do inherit,
Here thy praises I'll begin;
Here I raise my Ebenezer;
Here by thy great help I've come;
And I hope, by thy good pleasure,
Safely to arrive at home.

Jesus sought me when a stranger,
Wandering from the fold of God;
He, to rescue me from danger,
Interposed His precious blood;
How His kindness yet pursues me
Mortal tongue can never tell,
Clothed in flesh, till death shall loose me
I cannot proclaim it well.

O to grace how great a debtor
Daily I'm constrained to be!
Let thy goodness, like a fetter,
Bind my wandering heart to thee.
Prone to wander, Lord, I feel it,
Prone to leave the God I love;
Here's my heart, O take and seal it,
Seal it for thy courts above.

O that day when freed from sinning,
I shall see thy lovely face;
Clothèd then in blood washed linen
How I'll sing thy sovereign grace;
Come, my Lord, no longer tarry,
Take my ransomed soul away;
Send thine angels now to carry
Me to realms of endless day.

How Hymns Remind Us
of His Faithfulness

When my oldest daughter was born she was blue, which is okay for a Smurf but incredibly alarming for a newborn. Doctors and nurses stampeded into the delivery room, past me, and huddled around our daughter seconds after Maddie entered the world. I'd barely caught a glimpse of her in the doctor's hands, hadn't gotten to hold her, had no idea why all these turquoise scrubs rushed into our tiny room. All my body wanted to do was collapse, but even after nineteen hours of labor and delivery my senses were on high alert, heart racing, neck craning to see what they were doing to her, ears straining to understand the medicalspeak, desperate to find out what was wrong.

Praise God, after a few minutes, which felt like shuffled, confusing, fear-filled hours, the team suctioned our little girl's lungs and cleared her airways. Then she let out a piercing scream, which was the most beautiful music I've ever heard.

I'm grateful to say she's been breathing fine ever since.

Come, Thou Fount of every blessing, tune my heart to sing Thy grace.

My husband and I were thankful to the medical team and to God above that Maddie was okay, but we don't talk about it much anymore. She's twenty. She's a college athlete. And we've been through so many smiles and tears with her over the years that those opening measures of her life are sometimes forgotten. But I wonder what the cost is when I casually forget what God did for us in

Maddie's blue moment, that He gave her the gift of life, and us the gift of our daughter. I wonder if I've missed occasions where God would have been able to more fully remind me of His love, if only I'd kept the memory of this miracle more front and center.

Our fourth child came out breathing just fine, but at his one-week checkup our pediatrician detected a hole in his itty-bitty heart. He was referred to the children's hospital an hour away. We made arrangements for someone to watch our other three kids while we spent the day with pediatric cardiologists. They wrapped Maguire in a thick, warm blanket to lull him into a relaxed state and performed an ultrasound on his heart. Vivid greens, blues, and reds on the monitor indicated the whoosh of blood escaping the tiny hole in one of his ventricles.

The specialists told us Maguire had a structural heart problem that could either (a) develop as a "functional heart murmur," without any symptoms, or (b) require heart surgery—on our little guy who was only a handful of days old.

We had a follow-up in ten days. Those ten days were extremely long, trying to act like everything was normal, praying fervently, asking friends for prayers, trying not to freak out, freaking out anyway. My husband and I headed back to the hospital with Maguire. It was pouring down rain that day, the kind that you can barely see out the windshield. Traffic was miserable. Stop. Start. Stop. Start.

I felt sick from the thick, muggy scent of exhaust and all the jerky movements of the car, or maybe I felt sick from fear of what I might find out. We walked the same maze of hallways, endured again the deafening silence of elevators, the sterile scent clinging to the floors and walls, and another ultrasound.

Except this one revealed the hole in Maguire's heart had grown back together. It was completely, miraculously gone.

Streams of mercy, never ceasing, call for songs of loudest praise.

We wept in gratitude, snuggled our little guy extra close those next few days. But today? My twelve-year-old stands on a stage with yellow feathers stuck to a baseball cap perched on his head. He's blowing a buzzy kazoo in his role as one of Woodstock's friends in the musical *You're a Good Man Charlie Brown.* I sit in a theater seat during his dress rehearsal watching him up there, and I praise God that he's found his niche, that he's so full of life and joy. But how often do I even remember the hole-in-his-heart thing? So much has happened. Heck, this is Maguire's ninth play.

God has performed two giant miracles before my eyes. He saved my children's lives. Like real live Bible miracles. How do I ever lose sight of them?

What has God done for you?

Provided the check in the mail the same week you had an unexpected bill? Introduced you to someone who became a true friend or the perfect connection to find a roommate? Had your brakes perform better than they should have, stopping you within an inch of that other car? Orchestrated circumstances to land you the job you didn't know existed, but fit your skill set perfectly? When was the last time you thanked Him for those things?

Why do we forget the incredible ways God has been there for us? The ways He's saved us?

Prone to wander, Lord, I feel it, prone to leave the God I love.

As the apostle Paul confesses in his letter to the church in Rome, "I have the desire to do what is right, but not the ability to carry it out" (Romans 7:18 ESV).

How do we hold tight to all the ways God has provided for us?

Some of the folks in the Old Testament used rocks. Were they on to something?

In 1 Samuel 7 the nasty Philistine army advanced on the Israelites ready to attack. But God spoke with a voice like thunder totally disorienting the Philistines. They got all confused and the Israelites swept in and knocked them out, easy-peasy. This was major. God saved the Israelites, and they knew it.

The Israelite prophet Samuel did something that day to remember God and what He'd done. Samuel set up a monument, nothing fancy, he just used what he had—a rock. The word the Israelites used for this kind of memorial was *matzeveh*—think of it like a plaque or statue we'd erect today to mark a battle won, a hero buried, or the place where it all began. Samuel took this large stone, set it upright, like a fin, and named the stone Ebenezer (which means "stone of help").

Jacob did something similar after he wrestled with God—set a rock upright and poured oil on it to mark the spot—to help Jacob remember his crazy face-to-face encounter with God (Genesis 28:18). Moses also erected these matzevehs at the bottom of Mount Sinai (Exodus 24:4–6).

This is the pulse of the hymn "Come, Thou Fount of Every Blessing," written by Robert Robinson in 1758.[1] It is a monument in song to what God has done for us, a way to remind us of how He has helped us and saved us in the past, to reset our wandering hearts so we won't wander away from Him in the future.

Here I raise my Ebenezer; here by Thy great help I've come.

Do you have some sort of "Ebenezer" in your life— probably not a rock, but something you do to remember God's faithfulness?

Maybe you journal and highlight answered prayers in hot pink. Maybe there's a picture on your wall that reminds you of the home God provided or the moment you first met your spouse, and each time you see that photo you thank God for what He did. Perhaps you let your calendar prompt your praise—writing out gratitude lists near Thanksgiving; spending Advent, that season of anticipating Christmas, meditating on hope, love, joy, peace, and faith; and thanking God for freedom, and for the people who have fought for those rights around the Fourth of July.

Or maybe you're kind of random like me. Wanting to remember God, and thank God for all the things on all the days, but yet sometimes forgetting His faithfulness. Still questioning if He'll actually help one of my kids find the right college—one where they'll thrive and make good friends and stay close to Jesus. Or asking what in the world we'll do if my husband feels called to take that job he's been offered across the country. I try to remember God, but I forget and instead try to take these things into my own hands, wasting time fretting about outcomes that might not ever take place.

Prone to wander. Lord, I feel it.

But when I hear, "Come, Thou Fount of Every Blessing," I remember. It resets me.

This song is an Ebenezer for me. I don't hear it very often—it's not like it's playing at the gym. This old hymn is rarely on Christian radio, unless you happen to catch the beautiful remakes by Chris Tomlin or Shane & Shane. But sometimes you do. Or sometimes it randomly appears as a throwback on the set list at church. And it takes me back. I remember what God has done. I raise my hands as if raising my Ebenezer. Praising Jesus, because He rescued me from danger, how *His kindness yet pursues me.*

I rarely play CDs anymore because Spotify makes it so easy to have all my songs sorted on giant playlists. All I have to do is plug my phone into an auxiliary cord or enable Bluetooth and voilà, I have hours of my favorite music with no commercials. But one day a while back my dear friends, the Bundys, were releasing a new album. They gave me an advance copy of their CD, so I popped it into the player in my car and listened as I drove the familiar farm roads to pick up my kids from school.

I passed goats and fences, got stuck behind a tractor —*yikes*—and hung out in the pickup line at the front of school waiting my turn. I grumbled in my head about how slow that tractor drove. I felt the three o'clock weariness slip over me—the one that comes from rising each morning at six, moving full speed ahead until it's time to pick up the kids, then on the twenty-minute route to their school having my brain say, "Hey I'm tired." And my body answer, "Tell me about it."

I pulled up to the flagpole. My kids tumbled in. A few minutes of chatter about recess and homework, then they also fell victim to the afternoon weariness after a long day at school. The car got peacefully quiet with the music playing softly in the background. And as the final chords of an original song, "First Round," faded, the opening notes of "Come, Thou Fount of Every Blessing" came through the speakers.

The Bundys sing it a cappella with stunning harmonies, and a tingling crept up the back of my nose. Then the warmth of tears brimmed my eyes. I didn't know the sweet trio of siblings had recorded this hymn on their album.[2] And at the sound of it I remembered.

I remembered all of God's goodness. Not in flashes of specific memories. I didn't picture Maddie's lungs or Maguire's heart miracles. But I felt the fullness of it, of who God is, of all He's done to seize my heart. And in those moments nothing else mattered. The silly gripes and concerns evaporated as the remembering reset my soul. Because when I remember God, He's all I need and all I want. And I want to cling to that, remember it. Forever more.

Here's my heart, O take and seal it, seal it for Thy courts above.

CONTEMPLATE

Then Samuel took a stone and set it up between Mizpah and Shen. He named it Ebenezer, saying, "Thus far the LORD has helped us." (1 Samuel 7:12)

1. When was a time God did something amazing for you? Describe it:

2. How often do you remember what God did, and then go back and thank Him for it?

3. What will you use as your "Ebenezer" this week to recall how God has cared for you in the past?

6

IT IS WELL
WITH MY SOUL

Horatio Spafford, 1873

When peace like a river, attendeth my way,
When sorrows like sea billows roll;
Whatever my lot, thou hast taught me to say
It is well, it is well, with my soul.

It is well (it is well)
With my soul (with my soul)
It is well, it is well, with my soul.

Though Satan should buffet, though trials should
    come,
Let this blest assurance control,
That Christ has regarded my helpless estate,
And hath shed His own blood for my soul.

My sin—oh, the bliss of this glorious thought—
My sin, not in part but the whole,

Is nailed to the cross, and I bear it no more,
Praise the Lord, praise the Lord, O my soul!

For me, be it Christ, be it Christ hence to live:
If Jordan above me shall roll,
No pang shall be mine, for in death as in life
Thou wilt whisper thy peace to my soul.

But, Lord, 'tis for thee, for thy coming we wait,
The sky, not the grave, is our goal;
Oh trump of the angel! Oh voice of the Lord!
Blessed hope, blessed rest of my soul!

And Lord, haste the day when my faith shall be
    sight,
The clouds be rolled back as a scroll;
The trump shall resound, and the Lord shall
    descend,
Even so—it is well with my soul.

How Hymns Calm Our Storms

I have four children, but I've been pregnant five times.

I went to the bathroom and there was blood. So much blood. Bright scarlet blood. I called my doctor. They had me come in for a test. They would call me with results. Soon.

But soon didn't feel soon. Over 2,880 minutes later, yes, I was tracking time by minutes, I was heaping damp laundry in the dryer, a lavender-scented dryer sheet in one hand when they called.

"May I speak to Laura Smith?"

"This is."

"This is Heather from Dr. Eldridge's office." Heather. I still remember her name.

"Yes." My voice caught. I knew *why* she was calling. But I didn't know *what* she would say. And everything hinged on that *what.*

"Your blood work shows you are no longer pregnant."

The new washer and dryer of our starter home were shiny white. The walls, floors, and cabinets of the room were also bright white, clean, and fresh like laundry. But all I could think of was the blood. Too red. Too much. Shouldn't have been there.

As I type this more than eighteen years later, I still don't understand why Heather chose those words. Why didn't she say she was sorry? Why didn't Heather explain what happened? Why did the nurse refer to my pregnancy instead of my baby? And although I remember her name and her words, I don't remember mine. I don't remember responding. I don't remember hanging up. I barely remember the rest of that day.

I do know I fought to stay in control—to not break down, because it was so early in the pregnancy—no one except my husband and I even knew about it. We didn't know the gender. We never will. We hadn't picked out names. We hadn't planned our lives around this new baby. Yet.

I grew up in a household where we hid emotions, avoided conflict, and pretended the bad things didn't happen. As a girl I dealt with all the hard stuff on my own. And there were plenty of challenges to deal with. This is how I would handle this, too, by myself, without overreacting, without inviting my husband into the pain. Instead, I tried to shield him from it.

But that night in the dark of our room despite me trying to hold all the fragments together, beneath our thick down comforter with our ceiling fan whirring overhead, the uncontrollable sobs erupted. Brett held me close, his warm body cocooning mine, as I shook with sorrow, until my face was soaked, until no more tears came—tears for our baby we would never meet and the emptiness spreading inside me.

The author of "It Is Well With My Soul," Horatio Spafford, also experienced inexplicable loss of a child, but his was exponential.

Horatio Spafford's wife and four daughters were on an ocean liner on their way to Europe. Horatio needed to settle a few business items and then planned to join his family. But the ship went down. And all four of his daughters with it. His wife survived and sent him a telegraph with the tragic news. Spafford got on the next ship to join his despairing wife. He wrote this hymn on the voyage to find her.[1]

When peace like a river, attendeth my way, when sorrows like sea billows roll; whatever my lot, Thou hast taught me to say, It is well, it is well, with my soul.

How?

How did he write this?

After my miscarriage my brain ricocheted with unanswered questions. Why couldn't we have our baby? What had I done wrong? Was it because I'd been exercising? Stress? Something I had or hadn't eaten? Would we ever get pregnant again? Would our child have looked like me, or like Brett? Would he or she have been calm or feisty? Did this little one miss us? Because I missed our child so much, this sweet baby I never met. My heart felt like it was wrapped in barbed wire.

How on earth could Spafford sing that "peace" was attending him, that things were "well" with his soul or any other part of him? It feels impossible to breathe when you're encased in pain. Let alone sing.

But Jesus offers to pull us out of the swirling waves of despair, to calm our storms. If only we'll trust Him. This is what Horatio Spafford did and reminds us to do. His song has nudged countless people for about 150 years to do the same.

Christ has regarded my helpless estate.

For me it starts with this line. Jesus sees us. In our mourning and struggling. He saw me when that nurse called. He sees you when you tremble. He wants to take away all the angst and pain, heal it with His love, and replace it with peace.

I hate to type it out because I don't want to admit it. But somewhere in my darkest center after my miscarriage I asked, "If God loves me, why did our baby die?"

Christ . . . hath shed His own blood for my soul . . . Praise the Lord, praise the Lord, O my soul.

This next line takes me a step further. I think Jesus knew we'd have moments of doubt. Moments when loss feels so dark it's near impossible to see through. But

Jesus did something to help dispel our doubts, to help us comprehend the depths of His love even in despair. Jesus laid down His life for you and for me. He died on the cross not because He had to, but because He wanted to. Because He loves us that much, so inexplicably undeniably much. The apostle Paul reminds us of the vastness of Christ's love:

> And I pray that you, being rooted and established in love, may have power, together with all the Lord's holy people, to grasp how wide and long and high and deep is the love of Christ. (Ephesians 3:17–18)

Bethel Music's new take on this classic hymn adds new lyrics declaring the wind and waves know God's name.[2] We find this story about wind and waves in three of the four gospel accounts of Jesus's life (Matthew, Mark, and Luke). Interesting how for both the disciples and Horatio Spafford there was a boat, a storm, and a Savior.

Here it is from the book of Mark:

> A furious squall came up, and the waves broke over the boat, so that it was nearly swamped. Jesus was in the stern, sleeping on a cushion. The disciples woke him and said to him, "Teacher, don't you care if we drown?"
>
> He got up, rebuked the wind and said to the waves, "Quiet! Be still!" Then the wind died down and it was completely calm.
>
> He said to his disciples, "Why are you so afraid? Do you still have no faith?"

They were terrified and asked each other, "Who is this? Even the wind and the waves obey him!" (Mark 4:37–41)

If the elements that cause storms, literal and figurative in our lives know who Jesus is, obey Him, calm at the sound of His voice, it makes me believe stillness is possible for all of us. Even when the waves and storms surround us, or when the wind seems to blow everything the wrong direction, or when the salt water stings our eyes, Jesus has this, and everything else, under control. When we feel like we're drowning, gasping for air, Jesus doesn't just throw us a life preserver, He stops the storm.

Though trials should come, let this blest assurance control.

It's not always easy. The disciples were terrified in their storm and Jesus was physically sitting next to them. Still they asked, "Teacher, don't you care if we drown?"

And once again, Jesus showed them (and us) He does care. That when we are in danger He will and does act. It's just not always how we want it to happen. The Bible doesn't say what would have occurred if the disciples hadn't woken Jesus up, but I imagine He would have still protected them.

This gets tricky. If Jesus is in total control why did we lose our baby? Why did Horatio Spafford's daughters die? Why did you lose the person you love?

The answer is, I don't know.

God is so powerful and almighty, of course our human brains can't understand everything He does—the hows and the whys, even when we ache for answers. It's too complicated for us to understand. Oh, but we want to.

Yet here's the kicker: God knows exactly what we're experiencing. Because He watched His own son die a painful death. So if we question if God understands loss, the answer is, He does.

If we question if Jesus is in control, if He cares what happens to us, His question back to the disciples pins me to my seat: "Do you still have no faith?"

Do I?

Do you?

Even though God sent His only Son to die for us?

Even though Jesus willingly went to the cross and suffered for us?

Jesus understands pain and grief. He asks us to have faith in Him and His decisions, even when they hurt our human hearts, even when we can't make sense of them. He loves us so much, our Savior promises never to leave us:

> And surely I am with you always, to the very end of the age. (Matthew 28:20)

And with this statement from Jesus, the author of the book of Hebrews tells us:

> Since God assured us, "I'll never let you down, never walk off and leave you," we can boldly quote,
>
> > God is there, ready to help;
> > I'm fearless no matter what.
> > Who or what can get to me?
> > (Hebrews 13:5–6 MSG)

Which is logical. And how I want to live—assured and fearless.

Even when we feel alone or abandoned, even when we can't get our minds around painful circumstances, even when we wish things would have gone completely differently, this knowledge that the God of the universe, the God of angel armies is here, on our side, will not let us down, will never leave us, empowers us to be able to sing even in our darkest hours, "It is well with my soul."

We have this power, but sometimes it feels near impossible to tap into it. But even in the despairing times, if we stop trying to row ourselves with rubbery arms out of the thrashing of the squall and let Jesus take over, He can calm our storms. He can begin to heal us. We can live more fully in faith, and maybe even eke out a few notes from our hearts and mean them: *It is well (it is well), with my soul (with my soul). It is well, it is well, with my soul.*

CONTEMPLATE

And the peace of God, which surpasses all understanding, will guard your hearts and your minds in Christ Jesus. (Philippians 4:7 ESV)

May the God of hope fill you with all joy and peace as you trust in him, so that you may overflow with hope by the power of the Holy Spirit. (Romans 15:13)

1. Have you ever felt like you were drowning?

2. Write out one of the two verses from above and meditate on it.

3. Whenever the winds blow in your life this week, write them down here. Then recall Jesus halting that gale at sea. Finally, write over the "storms" you've written down, "It Is Well." If you need more space, feel free to grab an extra piece of paper and slip it in the book.

7

MY HOPE IS BUILT ON NOTHING LESS

Edward Mote, circa 1834

My hope is built on nothing less
Than Jesus' blood and righteousness;
I dare not trust the sweetest frame,
But wholly lean on Jesus' name.

> *On Christ, the solid Rock, I stand.*
> *All other ground is sinking sand;*
> *All other ground is sinking sand.*

When darkness seems to hide His face,
I rest on His unchanging grace.
In every high and stormy gale,
My anchor holds within the veil.

His oath, His covenant, His blood
Support me in the whelming flood;
When all around my soul gives way,
He then is all my hope and stay.

When He shall come with trumpet sound,
O may I then in Him be found,
Dressed in His righteousness alone,
Faultless to stand before the throne.

How Hymns Secure Us

My kids know the best route to get to the creek at the bottom of the 45-degree incline of our backyard, but they don't always use it.

If they first step on the smooth, bluish slate rock sticking out of the soil, and then onto the stone embedded in the earth next to it. If they grab the ginger-colored gnarled root of the ancient oak tree, then shift their weight to that bumpy stump cushioned with green springy moss, there are a series of footholds that lead them steadily down the hill along a secure pathway.

This is undeniably the best route. But they're kids. And they're impatient and adventurous. And this route takes longer as they embark on expeditions in our woods. Sometimes they want to forge their own trail, simply see if they can do it—if they can get down, or up, or both by themselves, without any "help" from the path nature has laid out for them. Sometimes they're just in a rush.

When my kids attempt a shortcut they often reappear at the house covered in mucky mud or with haphazard red scratches and scrapes on their knees and elbows or perhaps holding soaking wet shoes and soggy socks. Sometimes the thrill factor is worth it for them. But often there are lost balls, ripped sweatpants, and sometimes tears. They know the path is safer, more secure, particularly when it's muddy, snowy, or piles of soft leaves are underfoot and the slope is slick. Still, despite being unreliable and precarious, going off road sometimes appears quicker, easier, as if they forget there's a trail they can count on.

Similarly, when we're faced with the landslides of life, we know we can depend on Jesus, but sometimes we forget or try to do things on our own or simply grab onto the closest branch, instead of taking time to pray, ask Him for help, or read the Bible and remember who we are in Christ. Just like the path to our creek, our lives are filled with slippery slopes.

Has someone you trusted ever let you down? How did you feel? Confused? Shocked? Unsure how to react? Maybe as if the villain in a movie pulled a lever and the floor fell out below your feet? As you felt yourself falling did you reach out for a scheme to get back at that person? Or grab onto an opportunity to speak badly about them? When we're hurt and feel betrayed we can feel untethered, forget which way to go or what to do.

Have you ever been turned down for a job or had an idea you were passionate about get rejected? It feels personal sometimes, as if we, not our idea or résumé, were rejected. What did you reach for in that situation? Did you clamor to hold on to your dignity? Grab your past accomplishments? Backlash at whoever turned you down?

Is there that person in your life—you know, the one who makes you feel inadequate? When their name pops up on your phone, your pulse begins to race just thinking about what they might say, how they might make you feel. Do you go into fight or flight mode to protect yourself? Grit your teeth and prepare a snarky comeback before saying, "Hello." Or maybe choose to ignore the call altogether? These acts of self-preservation can slide us into saying something we'll regret or slip us out of a chance to stand up for something we believe in.

When we lose traction in life, we stumble and sometimes give in to a series of knee-jerk reactions. We slip and slide, skinning our knees and soaking our socks. But Jesus doesn't want us to flail. He offers a more stable solution. He talked about this to a crowd one day on a hillside near Capernaum. Jesus called it building our houses on solid rock—on Him.

> Anyone who listens to my teaching and follows it is wise, like a person who builds a house on solid rock. Though the rain comes in torrents and the floodwaters rise and the winds beat against that house, it won't collapse because it is built on bedrock. But anyone who hears my teaching and doesn't obey it is foolish, like a person who builds a house on sand. When the rains and floods come and the winds beat against that house, it will collapse with a mighty crash. (Matthew 7:24–27 NLT)

Storms slammed against the house. And it stood strong.

Because it was built on Jesus.

That's what I want. To stand strong. Even when the troubles of life come knocking at my door. That sounds way better than floundering for a foothold.

The hymn "My Hope Is Built on Nothing Less" reminds us of Jesus's talk with the crowd that day, specifically the familiar refrain, *On Christ, the solid Rock, I stand. All other ground is sinking sand; all other ground is sinking sand.* Are you singing yet?

The anthem "Cornerstone," from the popular worship band Hillsong, uses the first and last verses of "My Hope Is Built on Nothing Less" along with a few new lyrics of their own.[1] A spontaneous version of "Stand in Your Love," recorded by Josh Baldwin of Bethel Music, declares, *I am standing on the rock—my firm foundation.*[2] The bridge in "The Rock Won't Move" by Vertical Worship also pulls straight from this hymn.[3] Why are all these popular worship bands diving back into a hymn written in 1834 by Edward Mote?[4]

Because this hymn and its principle—that we need something to anchor ourselves to, or we start to slip—is a timeless truth. We, as a human race, just like my kiddos, are prone to grab onto faster, cheaper, easier, whatever everyone else is doing, past experiences, old habits— whatever's available when we lose our footing. We often search for a quick fix before turning to Jesus, hoping to find instant relief. But if we take a moment to secure ourselves in who we are in Christ, then we don't have to flail.

That person who disappointed us shouldn't make us fall flat. Because when we stand on the Rock, we feel

Him solid under our feet. Jesus never lets us down. Our relationship with Him is 100 percent secure, 100 percent of the time. His grace is constant. *When darkness seems to hide His face, I rest on His unchanging grace.*

When we get turned down or passed over, we don't have to struggle to prove ourselves. Because when we build our life on Jesus, we know in our hearts no position or role defines us. He does. We are His. Our identity is secure in Him. That opportunity may sound sweet, but not as sweet as the love of Christ. *I dare not trust the sweetest frame, but wholly lean on Jesus' name.*

And when the bully calls, even though that person might be brewing up a storm, we can swallow the taste of fear. We can bravely stand on solid footing, anchored in Jesus's strength, wind whipping through our hair, but not knocking us down. Because no matter what that person says, the King of the universe chooses us, says we are His beloved. *In every high and stormy gale, my anchor holds within the veil.*

My kids don't want the sting of a skinned knee. But some days they find themselves tumbling down the side of the hill and ending up battered.

I'm guessing none of us want our homes, careers, relationships, or families to collapse. So the question is: Are we building our "houses," our lives, on Jesus, the solid rock? Are we turning to Him first?

In the split second when we receive the jarring email or frustrating call, when we don't get what we want or what we hope for, when the walls of our house feel like they're crashing down, what is our instinct? Do we turn to Him? Do we plant our feet resolutely in Jesus—our firm foundation?

I long to stand like that. Firm. Unshakable. Steady. Fearless. Yes, I want that. But it's easy to get windblown in life's unexpected gales, and I often find myself teetering. I'm so grateful Jesus offers the strength and stability we could never find on our own. I want to intentionally proclaim, *On Christ, the solid Rock, I stand.* I want this to be my anthem when I'm succeeding and failing, climbing or falling, going toward something or away from it. I want a solid stance on the foundation I can trust, which will never ever crumble or let me down. *He then is all my hope and stay.*

If we build our houses on the solid bedrock of Jesus our King, choose strong, even bricks of the love and hope Christ offers, slop thick mortar of faith between them, then even when the Big Bad Wolf is standing right outside our doors huffing and puffing, we'll know the nastiest beast, nor anything else, can ever blow our houses down. We are secure. We are standing on solid rock.

CONTEMPLATE

Anyone who listens to my teaching and follows it is wise, like a person who builds a house on solid rock. Though the rain comes in torrents and the floodwaters rise and the winds beat against that house, it won't collapse because it is built on bedrock. (Matthew 7:24–25 NLT)

1. Has anything knocked you off your feet recently? What was your gut reaction on how to handle the situation? Would you have preferred to handle it differently?

2. How can you build your life on Jesus this week (commit to daily prayer, to reading a certain amount of the Bible, to attending church or a church-sponsored event) in order to better secure you when the next storm hits?

8

I LOVE TO TELL
THE STORY

A. Katherine Hankey, 1866

I love to tell the story of unseen things above,
Of Jesus and His glory, of Jesus and His love.
I love to tell the story, because I know 'tis true;
It satisfies my longings as nothing else can do.

> *I love to tell the story, 'twill be my theme in*
> *   glory,*
> *To tell the old, old story of Jesus and His love.*

I love to tell the story; more wonderful it seems
Than all the golden fancies of all our golden
    dreams.
I love to tell the story, it did so much for me;
And that is just the reason I tell it now to thee.

I love to tell the story; 'tis pleasant to repeat
What seems each time I tell it, more wonderfully
    sweet.

I love to tell the story, for some have never heard
The message of salvation from God's own holy
    Word.

I love to tell the story, for those who know it best
Seem hungering and thirsting to hear it like the
    rest.
And when, in scenes of glory, I sing the new, new
    song,
'Twill be the old, old story that I have loved so
    long.

How Hymns Stir Us

"I walked in that first day and the air was so humid I felt like I was trudging through rain clouds. The plastic chairs were all cracked, and the whole room reeked of rotten garbage. *Ew*!" My friend waves her hand in front of her face.

"Remember how dark it was? And the ceilings were so low, I had to duck," her husband laughs, brushing the top of his silvering hair as if he can feel the ceiling grazing it.

"I almost walked right back out," she says.

"I'm glad you didn't." He grins.

A warm autumn breeze flutters the pile of paper napkins sitting on our porch table. I take a bite of creamy Brie laced with sweet, gooey honey spread on a crisp cracker and lean forward in my Adirondack chair. I want to hear every detail of how my friends, who now live in New York City, first met when an unusual set of circumstances landed them both in Guatemala, in the same Spanish class, at the exact same time. Their facial expressions reveal they love telling this story as much as I love hearing it.

Do you remember the moment you met your spouse? Your first day on the job? When you went into labor?

We love to tell these stories—the stories about the turning points of our lives, when our hearts fluttered, our palms sweat, our worlds changed. Recalling these moments can be heartwarming or hilarious. They stir up feelings of excitement and love, and we long to share them with others.

What's your favorite story to share?

Kate Hankey's favorite story was about Jesus. She taught Bible studies to working-class girls in England in the 1800s, longing to share the life-changing love of Christ.[1] She also wrote the hymn "I Love to Tell the Story."[2]

There was another woman who did *not* like to tell stories. She was ashamed of her scandalous past involving multiple men. And so, she avoided bumping into neighbors, to limit the chances of having to explain herself or suffer people's stares and whispers. On a hot, dry day in her Middle Eastern town, she needed water. So she grabbed her earthen jar and went to the well about noon when no one would be there. She was surprised by an unexpected man traveling through town—Jesus.

Feeling worn out from his journey, Jesus was sitting by the well when the woman approached. He asked her for a drink. This was unheard of. No upright man would be seen speaking to *her*. Jesus knew all about her past, but that didn't stop Him from chatting. Jesus explained that He was living water. That all the things the woman had been searching for—ways to feel loved, complete, forgiven, accepted—there was a way to never thirst for these things again. The way was Him. He was the Messiah.

The woman was all stirred up by her encounter with Christ.

> The woman left her water jar beside the well and ran back to the village, telling everyone, "Come and see a man who told me everything I ever did! Could he possibly be the Messiah?" (John 4:28–29 NLT)

The woman didn't try to explain why she, the one who had been avoiding social interaction, was now out in the open. She didn't pretend to have all the answers. She was simply honest about who Jesus was for her. This encounter with Jesus transformed her life. And when we experience a life-changing moment, we want to share the story.[3]

I think if the hymn "I Love to Tell the Story" had been written back then, this woman would have sung it. Maybe she would have sung this particular stanza with extra gusto: *I love to tell the story, because I know 'tis true. It satisfies my longings as nothing else can do.*

Not far from the woman's town, there was a man who lived in caves. He ran around howling and cutting himself like a beast. His village tried to chain him up for his safety and theirs, but he busted through the chains time and time again.

And then the wild man met Jesus.

Jesus sent the evil spirits tormenting this man into a herd of pigs who went running down the hillside and into the lake. The man was free, safe, and calm—as if he were a completely new person.

The herdsmen who witnessed the transformation of the man (and of their pigs) were astounded. What they saw stirred them up, and they couldn't wait to tell the story.

> Those tending the pigs ran off and reported this in the town and countryside, and the people went out to see what had happened. (Mark 5:14)

That was just the herdsmen. But the man? The man who had been more like a wild animal and was now a normal guy? He wanted to stay and hang out with Jesus, with the One who had given him a new life.

> But Jesus said, "No, go home to your family, and tell them everything the Lord has done for you and how merciful he has been." So the man started off to visit the Ten Towns of that region and began to proclaim the great things Jesus had done for him; and everyone was amazed at what he told them. (Mark 5:19–20 NLT)

Perhaps this man would have sung these lines from the hymn at the top of his lungs as he visited those Ten

Towns: *I love to tell the story, it did so much for me. And that is just the reason I tell it now to thee.*

The people in the Bible who came in contact with Jesus didn't just walk but *ran* to tell their stories. Their lives were so completely and utterly changed they couldn't help but tell others the narrative of how they met Jesus, about what He said and did.

How has Jesus changed your life?

Is there a time when you felt dark or desperate, lonely or frightened, unloved or unseen, and Jesus picked you up and saved you?

Do you ever tell anyone about it?

Imagine if we strolled through the aisles of the grocery store pushing our carts with the squeaky wheels past bright red peppers and dark green spinach, so stirred up by what Jesus has done for us, we sang out loud, *I love to tell the story of unseen things above, of Jesus and His glory, of Jesus and His love.*

Okay, no one wants to hear me singing because I am sadly way off key. But you get the gist.

What if when we share the stories of how we met our spouses, we added in how only God could have arranged such a seemingly unlikely introduction. Or when we tell the tales about how we chose what school to attend or which job to take we explain how God intervened and closed this door or pointed us in that direction to make sure we got to the right place? Or what if we were truly brave and followed the example of the folks from the Bible who met Jesus? What if we rushed out telling everyone we encountered the stories of who Jesus is for us, of how He's changed us?

What if we told these stories over and over to show others how God is on the move? What if we also told these stories to remind ourselves of how He's been there for us time and time again—to stir up those memories of His goodness, kindness, and faithfulness throughout our lives? I don't know about you, but some days I crave those reminders.

Annie F. Downs says in her book *100 Days to Brave*, "When we're brave enough to share the God stories in our lives, it changes the people around us. It changes us to share them."[4]

Yes! I want positive, life-changing transformation for my family and friends who don't know Jesus or who are in a place of questioning. I want it for me too.

When we tell our own stories, we don't have to worry about getting them right or struggle to remember what order the events occurred. They're our stories. We know them best. The important parts ring loud and clear in our hearts. Why not share these beautiful stories of how Jesus has forever changed us with the world?

I love to tell the story, for those who know it best seem hungering and thirsting, to hear it like the rest.

CONTEMPLATE

The woman left her water jar beside the well and ran back to the village, telling everyone, "Come and see a man who told me everything I ever did! Could he possibly be the Messiah?" (John 4:28–29 NLT)

1. What's your favorite story to tell?

2. Jot down a story about how Jesus has changed your life. Then commit to sharing the story or another way Jesus has changed you, how He loves you, how He's there for you with someone else this week.

9

TAKE MY LIFE, AND LET IT BE

Frances Ridley Havergal, 1874

Take my life, and let it be
Consecrated, Lord, to thee;
Take my moments and my days,
Let them flow in ceaseless praise,
Let them flow in ceaseless praise.

Take my hands, and let them move
At the impulse of thy love;
Take my feet, and let them be
Swift and beautiful for thee,
Swift and beautiful for thee.

Take my voice, and let me sing
Always, only, for my King;
Take my lips, and let them be
Filled with messages from thee,
Filled with messages from thee.

Take my silver and my gold;
Not a mite would I withhold;
Take my intellect, and use
Every power as thou shalt choose.
Every power as thou shalt choose.

Take my will, and make it thine;
It shall be no longer mine.
Take my heart; it is thine own;
It shall be thy royal throne.
It shall be thy royal throne.

Take my love; my Lord, I pour
At thy feet its treasure-store.
Take myself, and I will be
Ever, only, all for thee.
Ever, only, all for thee.

How Hymns Help Us Live for Jesus

I love journals—their smooth covers decorated with polka dots, swirly water-colored flowers, or Bible verses in pretty raised lettering. Turning to a fresh page. Writing a heading in colorful ink. Watching my hand form curves and angles of letters that when assembled have meaning. There's excitement in the possibility of a blank page and how to fill it. Maybe it's the writer in me.

I feel the same potential each morning as I grab my Bible, pen, and journal. Still snuggled under my covers I write out truths, dreams, and prayers I want to infuse into my day. Another larger planner sits just to the left of my laptop on my desk. Thick ink lettering outlines my goals and action items for the week. And oh, the Calendar app. A quick glance each morning helps me manage all my obligations as well as the rehearsals, practices, and carpools for our kids.

I work best with routines. Knowing what happens next comforts me. Each line of each journal is an opportunity —a chance to plot a day pleasing to the Lord. It's good to be intentional, to prioritize time, and to stay focused. But no matter what we jot down, life is better when we openhandedly allow God to intervene. And although I try to control my schedule, God is the One who is truly in control and He always knows best. God takes what we put in our planner, and edits it to make our life stories more meaningful.

Sometimes God interrupts and throws my planner page completely out the window. The power might go out or someone comes down with a fever. But when God's plans feel like they're interfering, they're actually part of His bigger plan. That power outage might push us into needed rest. The sick kiddo might allow us the opportunity to pamper our sweetie with steaming peach tea, play a game of Yahtzee, or have a conversation we couldn't have shared if they'd been at school. A friend might message saying she'll be in town—could we grab lunch? Or an opportunity we'd never dreamed of may land in our inbox. But in order for God to use these opportunities, we need to be open to living our lives for Him. Are we willing to turn the pages over to Him?

The hymn "Take My Life," written by Frances Ridley Havergal in 1874,[1] feels like a journal entry. Her hymn reminds us how to live for Jesus, how to turn each day over to Him.

Take my moments and my days, let them flow in ceaseless praise.

What a great way to spend our days—in praise! But this isn't always easy. The days we have an argument, get a pounding headache, or our electricity bill shows up—way higher than expected. In those moments, it can be challenging to give thanks.

Yet, this is what God calls us to do, even if we'd prefer to schedule in some griping time. God is so good; He'll always provide something—a bird twittering, a thick pair of fuzzy socks, a sliver of moon hung in the sky as if placed perfectly on a hook to provide a soothing glow to the world. And as we begin looking for these samples of beauty, these touches of grace, we discover more and more things to thank our loving God for. Adding praise to our day becomes the perfect addition to our calendars.

Take my hands, and let them move at the impulse of Thy love. Take my feet, and let them be swift and beautiful for Thee.

The things our hands touch today—whether that's the fluffy head of a baby; sticky dough we're kneading into pizza crust; flat, smooth keys on a laptop, piano, or cash register; or maybe the firm handle of a toilet scrubber and a bottle of wicked strong bleach—let us touch these things because we love Jesus, because by doing the best we can with the work He's put in front of us, we're honoring

Him. The places our feet (or car) take us today—the tennis court, traffic court, our girlfriend's adorable stucco house at the end of a wooded court—let our feet go these places rooted strongly in our faith, determined to do what is right and good and just for God.

Take my voice, and let me sing always, only, for my King.

Take my lips, and let them be filled with messages from Thee.

I love to sing, but I believe the hymn refers to everything that comes out of our mouths—not just songs. We have a choice about what we say. We can build people up or tear them down. We can encourage and cheer or criticize and complain. The goal is for our words to sound like music to God.

But do they?

Because I have some things I'd really like to say during an evaluation, to a family member who's been grumpy, or to the customer service rep on the other end of the phone after being on hold for twenty-six minutes. Are these words melodious to God? Will we let Him interrupt our scheduled rants?

As King David sang,

May these words of my mouth and this meditation of my heart be pleasing in your sight. (Psalm 19:14)

Oh I want that. I want everything I say and think to be pleasing to God. But I mess up! I get frustrated by a referee's call, a politician's stance, an opinion that contradicts my own. Sometimes a thought flashes through my brain before I even see it coming. *Ugh.* I just want to swat the negativity away. I'm comforted that Jesus's brother, James, understood how difficult this is. He wrote:

> With the tongue we praise our Lord and Father, and with it we curse human beings, who have been made in God's likeness. Out of the same mouth come praise and cursing. My brothers and sisters, this should not be. (James 3:9–10)

This is something I'm working on. Something singing this hymn reminds me to keep trying to add into my days—positive words. All of us have challenges as we attempt to live for Jesus. The hymn addresses another issue many of us struggle with:

Take my silver and my gold; not a mite would I withhold.

Wait, how big is a mite anyway? Does this mean we have to take our entire paycheck and place it directly in the offering at church? No. *Whew,* because I was planning to spend it on my mortgage, groceries, and maybe that pretty new lipstick. But what a great reminder to give credit where credit is due, to remember God gave us the job, tax break, inheritance, or funding that gave us all the financial resources we have. When we open our checkbook or bank app, let's dedicate it to God saying, "Here's your ledger, God. Add and subtract as you see fit."

As James also said:

> Whatever is good and perfect is a gift coming down to us from God our Father. (James 1:17 NLT)

So if God gave us the resources of hands, feet, voice, days, words, and money, how are we going to use them?

The apostle Paul sums it up for the church in Rome like this:

> Take your everyday, ordinary life—your sleeping, eating, going-to-work, and walking-around life— and place it before God as an offering. (Romans 12:1 MSG)

Of course Jesus wants us to do the big things for Him—work the job He's called us to, marry someone who helps us follow the Lord well, but He also calls us to spend each ordinary, everyday moment living for Him. This could mean praying over your husband while you fold his laundry, or even though you're in a rush, stopping to help the elderly woman load her groceries into her car. It means making all the things—not just the big things or the churchy things—an offering to Jesus.

Yet, I still hold on to what I hope to accomplish. Do you? It's so satisfying writing something down in my planner, then placing a solid check mark next to it. But when we clutch our hands, there's no room for God to take things out that don't belong or to pour anything new into our lives that would be better, more amazing than our limited vision can imagine.

I get this wrong too often.

And so, I am grateful God gives us the opportunity daily to turn the page to a blank piece of paper—to hand Him our pens (you can use pencil, or your Notes app if you prefer), and let Him write out another glorious page of the story He has planned for us all along.

Take myself, and I will be ever, only, all for Thee.

CONTEMPLATE

Take your everyday, ordinary life—your sleeping, eating, going-to-work, and walking-around life—and place it before God as an offering. (Romans 12:1 MSG)

1. Jot down some things you have scheduled for this week (this could be appointments, how you'll spend money, conversations you'll have, workouts, meals you have planned, etc.). Which of these to-dos do you find hardest to turn over to God?

2. Listen to "Take My Life" and ask God what in your life He'd like for you to try to turn over to Him this week?

10

BE THOU MY VISION

Based on an Irish poem attributed to Dallan Forgaill
Translated from Old Irish by Mary Elizabeth Byrne in 1905
Versified by Eleanor Hull in 1912

Be thou my vision, O Lord of my heart;
Naught be all else to me, save that thou art.
Thou my best thought, by day or the night,
Waking or sleeping, thy presence my light.

Be thou my wisdom, and thou my true Word;
I ever with thee and thou with me, Lord;
Thou my great Father, I thy true son;
Thou in me dwelling, and I with thee one.

Be thou my battle shield, sword for the fight;
Be thou my dignity, thou my delight;
Thou my soul's shelter, thou my strong tower:
Raise thou me heavenward, O Power of my power.

Riches I heed not, nor man's empty praise,
Thou mine inheritance, now and always:

Thou and thou only, first in my heart,
High King of heaven, my treasure thou art.

High King of heaven, my victory won,
May I reach heaven's joys, O bright heaven's Sun!
Heart of my own heart, whatever befall,
Still be my vision, O Ruler of all.

How Hymns Help Us Fight Our Battles

"Pick your battles" is advice often given when dealing with a difficult coworker or when raising kids. But we rarely have the luxury of picking our battles. It seems more often than not, our battles pick us.

We're budgeting—saving for those adorable chairs made of reclaimed wood, staying within our spending limits, then *wham* our hot water heater goes out. And it costs hundreds of dollars to replace. All of a sudden we're in a battle. And it's not just the expense that gets us. We're angry the stupid thing went out. Frustrated it will take the plumber four days to repair because that's a lot of icy cold showers and only cleanish clothes. We're aggravated that the money we'd been diligently saving to buy the perfect chairs for our kitchen is now going toward something no one, including us, will ever *ooh* and *ahh* over, let alone see.

Or maybe we've done a stellar job avoiding the person who pushes our hot buttons. We even deleted her from our social media accounts because it's safer that way. Then at the school carnival, there she is, working the booth with us. Really? She makes a snide comment. Then masks an insult about our weight with a false compliment about our "slimming" outfit. She throws in a remark about the award her son earned, knowing full well our child did not receive the same accolade. We bite our tongues. Redirect the conversation. Check the clock. But we're sitting on a battlefield. One we did not sign up for.

Or perhaps we've been exercising willpower over that thing we consume that we know is bad for us. We all have different vices. And we know better about this one. So we haven't purchased it. Don't have it in our house. But we're at a neighborhood cookout. Everyone's outside. It's dark. It's late. The kids are all running around waving sizzling sparklers like magic wands leaving glowing streams in the air. Others who maybe don't have a problem with said thing are partaking and enjoying it, plus no one would probably notice. We're in a battle of willpower, of recognizing what's best for others isn't always best for us, of honoring our bodies because God made them, of saying no to something we know we enjoy for a hot second (even if the endgame turns out badly every single time).

How do you fight your battles? I only named three that came to mind in a heartbeat. There are much harder things to deal with—losing your phone with all your contacts, photos, and even your credit card tucked in the pouch on the back; losing a job; losing someone you love. How do you fight those battles?

C. S. Lewis wrote an entire novel, *The Screwtape Letters*, about a demon assigned to picking battles with a human he's assigned to.[1] The demon, Wormwood, writes letters to his uncle, Screwtape. Wormwood reports he distracted his human from listening to a sermon by making him smell the oniony breath of a man near him in church, and he fills his human's head with thoughts of uncertainty. Lewis's book is an illustration of how we're under attack all day long. Not by our bank account or that person who drives us crazy or even ourselves, but by a battle taking place in the heavenly places.

> Put on the full armor of God, so that you can take your stand against the devil's schemes. For our struggle is not against flesh and blood, but against the rulers, against the authorities, against the powers of this dark world and against the spiritual forces of evil in the heavenly realms. (Ephesians 6:11–12)

Okay, that sounds a bit scary.

Until we remember Jesus has already won—already defeated Satan. Before you panic, breathe that in.

But if our battles are truly in the heavenly realms, how do we fight them? First, by realizing that our real enemy is the Enemy. And if that's who we're up against, then we're going to need to pull in help from the strongest warrior around.

"Be Thou My Vision," a hymn originally written as a Celtic poem around AD 700 to honor Saint Patrick,[2] gives us some wise and clear instructions on how to fight our battles.

Thou my best thought, by day or the night, waking or sleeping, Thy presence my light.

Thou my best thought. Basically that's it. Because when our best thought is Jesus, we remember He's better than those chairs we wanted to buy. Sure, they'd look great in our kitchen, but they're not critical to our happiness. When our best thought is Jesus, we understand that even though a certain someone gets under our skin like a rash, Jesus loves us, and that's what truly counts. When Jesus is our best thought, we realize that tempting tidbit will never truly satisfy, only Jesus can and will. When everything but Jesus is *naught to us,* we can remember He already won this battle. All we need to do is stick with Him.

Great. So we're calling on God, looking at Him, putting Jesus front and center, but that bill, that person that hurts our feelings, or that mesmerizing morsel (feel free to insert a vice that takes you over the top) is right in front of us. We could reach out and touch it. Maybe we're already touching it. Now what?

The apostle Paul explains to the church of Ephesus that when these battles rage, because they will rage, we need to

> put on the full armor of God, so that when the day of evil comes, you may be able to stand your ground, and after you have done everything, to stand. Stand firm then, with the belt of truth buckled around your waist, with the breastplate of righteousness in place, and with your feet fitted with the readiness

that comes from the gospel of peace. In addition to all this, take up the shield of faith, with which you can extinguish all the flaming arrows of the evil one. Take the helmet of salvation and the sword of the Spirit, which is the word of God. (Ephesians 6:13–17)

"Be Thou My Vision" virtually echoes these words. For me it's sometimes easier to remember songs than Scripture. If that's true for you, you might want to keep this hymn handy. It reminds us to put on the armor of God, yup His armor. It protects and helps us diffuse the enemy's futile attempts against us.

Be thou my battle shield, sword for the fight; be thou my dignity, thou my delight.

That person I struggle with, really struggle. It's because I feel they rob me of my value. But they don't really. God already says we're His heirs, His treasures. Yet, I allow that person's opinion about my hair or weight or the achievements of my offspring measure my worth, deflate my pride. Which is ridiculous, but I do it anyway.

And the thing I crave? I try to rationalize that it tastes good to me, calms me, that I deserve it. Why do I think little old me deserves things I know in my heart I shouldn't have? That's just nonsense.

Those chairs (or any home decor, shade of nail polish, or buttery-soft leather purse) are things that make me feel better about myself. Sometimes I want them because they're pretty, because they're desirable to look at and touch. And that's great, fun even. God wants us to delight in the things He gives us. But sometimes I want those things in hopes that when other people see those things, they might "think" better of me. *Ugh.*

So my favorite line from "Be Thou My Vision" is, *Riches I heed not, nor man's empty praise.*

Because praise from man is empty.

Yet, we crave it, don't we? We crave likes on social media, and compliments on our homes, outfits, and meals we prepare. We want to have the clever response at book club and be able to recite an applicable verse from memory at Bible study.

Why?

So we can proudly strut our stuff and feel like we matter.

But here's the secret. We do matter. To God. Not because of our achievements or furniture. Because of Jesus. So, I cling to this lyric, *nor man's empty praise.* And I sing it in my head when I'm under attack.

We can choose to get distracted by the world. Or we can focus on Jesus; have Him be our best thought.

When we do that we can fight our battles. We can find more strength than we have on our own, more willpower, patience, focus, stamina, and courage. We can put on the shoes of peace, buckle up the belt of truth, strap on the breastplate of righteousness, set the helmet of salvation on our heads, hold out the shield of faith, and wield the sword of the Spirit, while we sing, *High King of heaven, my victory won, may I reach heaven's joys, O bright heaven's Sun!*

And when we sing, we can be assured that we're surrounded by God's love. His angel armies are on *our* side.

We are safe, protected, and can win our battles thanks to the *High King of heaven . . . O Ruler of all.*

===== CONTEMPLATE =====

Put on the full armor of God, so that when the day of evil comes, you may be able to stand your ground. (Ephesians 6:13)

1. What battles are you fighting in this season?

2. How do you think envisioning Jesus by your side the next time you're confronted could help you fight a battle? Write out the scenario of how it would look different than a time you tried to fight the same battle on your own.

11

JESUS PAID IT ALL

Elvina M. Hall, 1865

I hear the Savior say,
"Thy strength indeed is small;
Child of weakness, watch and pray,
Find in me thine all in all."

Jesus paid it all,
All to Him I owe;
Sin had left a crimson stain,
He washed it white as snow.

For nothing good have I
Whereby thy grace to claim,
I'll wash my garments white
In the blood of Calvary's Lamb.

And now complete in Him
My robe His righteousness,
Close sheltered 'neath His side,
I am divinely blest.

Lord, now indeed I find
Thy power and Thine alone,
Can change the leper's spots
And melt the heart of stone.

When from my dying bed
My ransomed soul shall rise,
"Jesus died my soul to save,"
Shall rend the vaulted skies.

And when before the throne
I stand in Him complete,
I'll lay my trophies down
All down at Jesus' feet.

How Hymns Cleanse Us

I open my fridge countless times a day, but I seem to avoid some of the messes in there. I look for the almond milk to add a creamy splash to my coffee, the leftover half of my burrito bowl to heat up for lunch, the blackberries, or the chocolate syrup. I buy most of the groceries and put them away, so I usually know where the lesser used items are—the maraschino cherries, the sweet and spicy Thai sauce. Yet I will go weeks, okay, sometimes months, without being aware of the gunk and goo that seems to spawn across the shelves and in the bottoms of the drawers.

Today I noticed. Our fruit drawer is typically crammed full, but when I pulled out some grapes for the kids' breakfast, the only thing left was an old lime. Pitiful. And in the emptiness of the drawer I noticed two smushed grapes, a variety of crumbs (what fruit has crumbs?), and what appeared to be shriveled pieces of lettuce. Not sure how they migrated from the vegetable drawer, or if they actually used to be lettuce. Hard to say.

Since it was virtually empty, I removed the drawer. Beneath it were more crumbs, something dark and sticky—syrup?—and three of those white plastic things that hold the top of a bread bag together, plus some other ick. *Ew.* I composted the grayish lime, and filled the drawer with warm, sudsy water to soak. Then I went to work with a scrubber on the fridge. How could I be looking around the fridge daily and not see this gunk?

The pathetic part? As soon as the drawer was put back in place, mostly clean (except for the bright red stain on the bottom I scrubbed and scrubbed, which could be the juice of a retired raspberry), I noticed how gross the vegetable drawer was. And to be honest, I just didn't have the time or energy to take on its cleansing today.

I think my life is like that sometimes too. I'm living it day after day, but in the midst of doing I fail to see the grime and yuck forming a thin layer on all my surfaces. My family must get frustrated by my desire to do things *my* way time and time again. Acquaintances might feel I'm unfriendly because as an introvert I tend to keep to myself. I judge others. I'm prideful. Sometimes I'm so focused on trying to accomplish something, I fail to see how what I'm doing might affect or offend someone else.

Since it took some serious elbow grease, several ounces of cleaner, and a wad of paper towels to get my refrigerator drawer and surface cleaned, when I make the realization that my life needs some spring cleaning, I assume it will also take an indescribable amount of work. And sometimes that feels daunting. Like I don't even want to start.

But that's not how it goes with Jesus. We don't have to scrub until our arms are sore. He already washed us clean. The refrain of the hymn "Jesus Paid It All" by Elvina Hall captures His cleansing power.

Jesus paid it all, all to Him I owe. Sin had left a crimson stain (much like that raspberry), *He washed it white as snow.*

White as snow.

I love the fact that Jesus cleans me up, because I am so incapable of doing this on my own. I can't even keep my fridge clean; how could I possibly keep my heart clean? For my day-to-day transgressions it's easy to confess my mistakes, and receive His grace. After talking to Jesus about my mishaps I feel all shiny.

But the really thick, sticky sins of my past? They haunt me. Yes, I've handed them over to Jesus. Yes, my brain knows He forgives *all* my sins, not just the surface grime, the stuff in the drawer, but also the deep stains, the stuff festering under the drawer of my heart, like raspberry juice. But my heart struggles to fully accept this. Because I don't deserve to be forgiven. And, because sometimes I fail to forgive myself.

In Nicholas Sparks's novel *The Last Song,* two girls meet on a North Carolina beach. As the girls get to know one another, one asks, "So what's the worst thing you've ever done?"[1]

Just reading this dialogue makes me squirm. I hope no one ever asks me that question out loud. Because when I think of the worst things I've done, well, I wish they weren't part of my personal soundtrack. Do you have any of these things?

I wish I could go back and tell the college-aged Laura to go home, to walk out, to say no, to get a grip. I'm embarrassed and ashamed by my actions. But as the sins of my past try to haunt me all over again, *I hear the Savior say, "Thy strength indeed is small. Child of weakness, watch and pray, find in Me thine all in all."* And I am transported from disdain for myself, to love for my Jesus.

I'm reminded that I *am* lacking and weak, but He has strengthened me, enabled me to walk away from the dark past and into the bright future. Jesus reminds us that He has paid it *all.* Not some. His blood didn't just wash away our snide comments or how impatient we were standing in line at the airport. His blood washed away the "worst" things, too, just as clean, just as completely.

But we need to 100 percent believe that.

Do you believe it? That Jesus forgives your ugliest moment?

We need to truly let it sink in that Jesus is our all in all, that He not only has the power to wash away the very worst of our sins, but He uses that power, has used it, has bleached our sins so pure white, it's like they never even happened. Like we never even walked into those places, thought those thoughts, or did those things.

When I let this truth penetrate my soul, I want to stop hiding and stuffing and stashing all of my past sins, pull them out, take each and every one of them to Jesus, and beg Him to scrub me clean. Because *nothing good have I whereby Thy grace to claim, I'll wash my garments white in the blood of Calvary's Lamb.*

What sweet relief. What freedom.

If I don't have to carry around the heaviness of my past, I can go back to living my life again. Well, sort of. Because how I do life on the days when I'm not paying attention to this glorious thing Jesus has done for me, isn't the same as the days when I am fully aware of how powerful He is, how lavish Jesus is with grace. What complete cleansing power He has, and how that free, undeserved scrub-down makes all the difference. Yes, it means in the end we can all stand before Jesus's throne, *in Him complete,* But it also means every day, any day, where old habits and temptations rear their heads, or past mistakes stalk our consciences, I'll repeat it over and over, *Jesus paid it all.* Those sins have no power over us. Zero. Zip.

My fridge will need to be cleaned again. Soon. Who am I kidding? The veggie drawer needs to be cleaned right now. But our mistakes? Once Jesus washes them clean, there's no need to go back in again for past sins with more cleaning supplies and scrubbers. His pressure wash is permanent. Yes, new sins will pop up, like the piece of pasta that falls off a plate in the back of the fridge or the cilantro that turns to mush. And just like we need to go back into the fridge and clean up the new messes, we need to hand Jesus our latest little white lies and acts of selfishness. But once they're clean, they're clean. That's it. Game up.

Jesus never runs out of grace. He never decides He's sick of cleaning up after us. As long as we take our spots to Him, He'll wash them white as snow. I love Kristian Stanfills's modern take on this hymn where he repeats that line over and over with an accompanying guitar rift emphasizing how clean, how pure, how complete Jesus's grace makes us.[2] Dazzling white.

All to Him I owe. Sin had left a crimson stain. He washed it white as snow.

CONTEMPLATE

Though your sins are like scarlet, they shall be as white as snow; though they are red as crimson, they shall be like wool. (Isaiah 1:18)

1. Do you have anything in your past you wish you could erase?

2. Write "Jesus paid it all" over any of those past transgressions you listed above. Come back to this page throughout the week retracing, or writing over "Jesus paid it all" each day.

12

WHAT A FRIEND WE HAVE IN JESUS

Joseph M. Scriven, 1855

What a Friend we have in Jesus, all our sins and
griefs to bear!
What a privilege to carry everything to God in
prayer!
O what peace we often forfeit, O what needless
pain we bear,
All because we do not carry everything to God in
prayer.

Have we trials and temptations? Is there trouble
anywhere?
We should never be discouraged; take it to the
Lord in prayer.
Can we find a friend so faithful who will all our
sorrows share?
Jesus knows our every weakness; take it to the
Lord in prayer.

Are we weak and heavy laden, cumbered with a
load of care?
Precious Savior, still our refuge, take it to the Lord
in prayer.
Do your friends despise, forsake you? Take it to
the Lord in prayer!
In His arms He'll take and shield you; you will
find a solace there.

Blessed Savior, thou hast promised thou wilt all
our burdens bear
May we ever, Lord, be bringing all to thee in
earnest prayer.
Soon in glory bright unclouded there will be no
need for prayer
Rapture, praise and endless worship will be our
sweet portion there.

How Hymns Comfort Us

When Jamie and Tine (short for Christine) both moved
into my neighborhood in fifth grade, we thought we'd
be best friends the rest of our lives. We walked to school
together every day—in the mornings sharing any drama
that happened in our homes since the afternoon before,
and on the way home swapping all the conversations and
situations that occurred at school. We played endless
hours of Monopoly in Tine's clubhouse, raised rabbits,
rode bikes, did each other's hair and nails, played kick
the can, street hockey, Legos, and listened to the Beatles.

But in high school Jamie cheered and played soccer. Tine swam and ran cross-country. And I danced. We stayed friends but didn't see each other as much due to varying, busy schedules. And when drama happened at my house or during my school day, they weren't always the first ones to hear about it. Sometimes they never heard about it. I missed Jamie's and Tine's ears, their perspective, the open, honest relationship we'd built.

But even in that empty space, I still had someone I could talk to. Not an imaginary friend or one of my stuffed animals, but Jesus. He was never too busy, never with another group of friends. *Can we find a friend so faithful, who will all our sorrows share?*

Jamie remains one of my dearest friends today, but sadly I see her only once or twice a year. Tine, I still adore and hope all of the happiness for, but the only time I see her is on social media. These were the people I swore I'd tell all my secrets and share all of my triumphs with forever. But people move and life changes. Who were your BFFs when you were ten? How often do you talk to them now?

When my oldest daughter was two, we moved back to Ohio. I met a group of crazy, brilliant women who also had two-year-old daughters. We basically lived in each other's homes, rotated houses for play dates, met at the pool every single summer day, formed a book club, hosted dinner parties, carved pumpkins, watched fireworks, and even folded laundry together. I can still taste an amazing layered-salad with blue cheese and dried cherries we all ate one day while the kids gobbled mac and cheese at a plastic table nearby. I can still feel the silkiness of a peacock feather I found at the old farmhouse one of the women was making into a beautiful home for her family. One woman was a mastermind at math, another the best cook I've ever met (*double the cheese in every recipe*, she insisted). One friend could organize a party fit for the Grammy Awards. Another was one the most creative souls I've encountered. I learned so much from them. For sure we would watch our beautiful girls grow up, learn to drive, go to prom together. Except for one mama-daughter combo who moved an hour away, another across the country. There was a heartbreaking fallout with one lady that to this day confuses and saddens me. And the other mama went back to work full-time while I stayed at home. None of the girls even ended up attending the same elementary school, let alone the same prom. And although at the time I turned to these women for all of my questions about potty training, pregnancy, page-turners, and piecrusts, I now turn to them for nothing. I do still pray that the women and their daughters are filled with joy.

The dissolving of this mama club was no one's fault. No one planned for it to happen. It just organically faded. We live in a transient town and life is a whirlwind. As we grew apart, I missed the ease, the sharing, but I was never alone. *Do your friends despise, forsake you* (or move away, or drift apart)? *Take it to the Lord in prayer!*

Relationships. Even the ones that stick, that stay, they're complicated, aren't they? We might have a couple of friends we feel comfortable talking to about our faith, another who has great advice on eating healthy and ways to fit exercise into our lives, yet another group of friends might be the parents on our kids' sport team, and all things about the game, tournaments, and coaching can be discussed with them. There are a few friends who truly understand our work. But it's rare that we find one friend who we can go to with all of these topics.

My best friend is my husband. He knows me better than anyone else on earth. He'll listen to all of my stuff, even if it's something he doesn't quite get, or want to get—like how much I love my new mascara or the novel I'm reading set in France. But even though I believe God made us for each other, there are days where we feel like we're talking past each other, like we're both speaking different languages and not even understanding where the other person is going. It's not that we don't care or don't have context, it's just that we're human, and we're not the same human.

Who are your best friends? Have you always known them? How many friends do you have that you could share everything with and know they would understand you? Have you ever lost a friendship or had a falling out with a family member? Who do you go to when you are sad and excited and won the lottery or lost your keys? Who do you talk with about the grudge you're striving to let go of and the learning disability one of your kids is struggling with? Who do you ask if you should apply for that position or date that man or stay home because you feel really crummy, but you know people are counting on you?

What about when that person doesn't answer your calls or texts, fails you, leaves?

Joseph Scriven knew what it was like to lose the relationships he counted on for counsel and love. The night before his wedding, his fiancée drowned. Later, Joseph moved, fell in love again, and got engaged. In 1855, his new fiancée died of an illness before they ever walked down the aisle. Such tragedy. That same year, he wrote the hymn "What a Friend We Have in Jesus," interestingly not to comfort himself, but his mother.[1] *Are we weak and heavy-laden, cumbered with a load of care? Precious Savior, still our refuge.*

I can't imagine the anguish and loneliness Scriven was cumbered with. And, still, he knew Jesus was his refuge. Because Scriven learned in the midst of his pain that although relationships might fail us, Jesus never will. When we don't know where else to go, when the things we want most are unspeakable, when the person we want to share with is unavailable, Jesus will always listen. We can take all of our needs all of the time to our very best friend, Jesus, in prayer.

I'm not saying Jesus is our backup. He's actually the first one we should go to. He's the One who gently wakes us in the morning after providing us with the miracle of restorative sleep. He provides us with all our needs, stands by us always, and wants us to talk to Him, about, you guessed it, everything! Anything you would ask or share with your best friend or soul mate? Jesus wants you to talk it over with and communicate it with Him. As the song says, *May we ever, Lord, be bringing ALL to Thee in earnest prayer.*

That's the cool thing about Jesus. He's the best friend when we're ten and playing kickball with the neighbor kids, and our best friend as we enter adulthood and jobs and marriage and raising a family. He's our best friend when we're healthy or sick, relaxed or stressed, energized or exhausted. Jesus never moves away, becomes distant, gives up on us, or lets us down. When Jesus appeared to the disciples after the resurrection He said, "I am with you always, even to the end of the age."

Always. Even to the end. *What a friend we have in Jesus.*

CONTEMPLATE

And surely I am with you always, to the very end of the age. (Matthew 28:20)

1. Have you ever lost a friend or felt lonely? How did that make you feel? Describe below.

2. How often do you turn to Jesus as your best friend?

3. What will you take to Jesus in prayer this week? Why not start now—write out something you want to talk to Him about and then pray the words out loud every day this week.

13

ROCK OF AGES

Augustus Toplady, 1776

Rock of Ages, cleft for me,
Let me hide myself in thee;
Let the water and the blood,
From thy wounded side which flowed,
Be of sin the double cure;
Save from wrath and make me pure.

Not the labor of my hands
Can fulfill thy law's demands;
Could my zeal no respite know,
Could my tears forever flow,
All for sin could not atone;
Thou must save, and Thou alone.

Nothing in my hand I bring,
Simply to the cross I cling;
Naked, come to thee for dress;
Helpless look to thee for grace;

Foul, I to the fountain fly;
Wash me, Savior, or I die.

While I draw this fleeting breath,
When mine eyes shall close in death,
When I soar to worlds unknown,
See thee on thy judgment throne,
Rock of Ages, cleft for me,
Let me hide myself in thee.

How Hymns Protect Us

There weren't many people around as my oldest daughter, Maddie, and I ran through Central Park. It was cloudy and 40 degrees, but we were on a special mother/daughter trip celebrating her upcoming high school graduation and didn't care. We jogged the pathways, stopped at a pond to stroke the slick, hard shells of baby turtles, and meandered past a small handful of giggling children frolicking around the Alice in Wonderland statue. We climbed the tower of Belvedere Castle to take in the view, and as we descended saw a streak of lightning. It was accompanied by deep and growly thunder. Moments later the sky opened and we were in the midst of a downpour.

Side note, neither Maddie nor I have any sense of direction. But we both remembered passing the Met on the east edge of the park. We were excited to explore inside, but were saving it as the destination of our run—a reward for a nice workout. We knew if we ran that way, we'd bump into it. It's pretty big. So, we took off, sprinting up and

111

down staircases, under bridges, laughing at our predicament. Out of breath, I strained to keep up with Maddie's athletic, teenage legs. After a few minutes, we got to the museum, but it looked different. And said, "American Museum of Natural History" on the front, which in any language does not translate to Metropolitan. So we did what you do in New York.

We asked a hot dog vendor, "Where is the Met?" We assumed it must be just up or down the street. If you're a New Yorker, you're cracking up right now. As was the hot dog guy.

"Straight across the park (say 'park' in your best New York accent)." He pointed while squirting thick, yellow mustard on a dog.

"No," we corrected him. "The Metropolitan Museum of Art. Isn't it just down the street?"

Now he was annoyed. He shook his head, slid a hot dog in a steamed bun, and passed it to a tiny woman with a headscarf. "It's on the Eastside. You're on the Westside." He didn't add the descriptor "idiots," but it was implied.

By now our skin was soaked. Rain rolled over our eyelashes and into our eyes. The metallic taste drowned our tongues. Maddie and I half-cried, half-laughed out of frustration, and at our malfunctioning inner compasses.

We headed back into the trenches to cross to the other side of the park. The rain was unrelenting, alternating pelting our backs or faces, depending on which way the path curved.

We told each other, "Almost there," and asked, "You doing okay?"

The lightning seemed to flash every minute. Each step seemed to fall in a puddle, sopping our feet. Without verbalizing it Maddie and I both secretly worried about our well-being in the middle of stormy Central Park. No one knew we were there. What if one of us slipped? What if we were mugged?

And even though our legs were dead, and I was out of breath, when we finally spied the museum we sprinted up the white granite steps and into the vestibule. Immediately our shoulders released the tension we'd been holding. We attempted wiping our faces with soaking wet sleeves and took a minute for breathing and shivering and reorienting ourselves. But after a moment or two safely out of the storm and in a dry warm place, we broke into hysterics, able to laugh at our predicament and each other's lovely drowned-rat appearances.

We bought tickets from the machine and proceeded to marvel at how Seurat used pointillism, the arrangements of multitudes of dots, to illustrate vibrant circus scenes. We tangibly felt the freedom evoked by Calder's mobiles composed of floating red metal shapes. Once out of the storm our experiences were no longer sculpted by the inclement weather. We were liberated from the discomfort and anxiousness. We'd found a safe cleft. And it changed everything.

You don't hear the word *cleft* very often, but it's in the hymn "Rock of Ages." In fact, it's my favorite part of the hymn. The old language of hymns sometimes trips us up or causes us to disengage because a word like *cleft* might go in one ear and out the other. At least it did mine. For ages. Get it? But a cleft is a safe spot, like the vestibule of the Met after you've been lost in a storm. And this is what Jesus is for us—our safe spot.

When I searched Spotify to see if any modern bands had done a revamp of the hymn "Rock of Ages," I saw the entire list of numbers from the hit musical *Rock of Ages*, which has nothing to do with Jesus and everything to do with rock and roll. My search also brought up way too many versions of the song by the same name by Def Leppard. In that "Rock of Ages" the glam metal band asks over and over again, "What do you want?"[1]

What *do* you want?

Good question.

What do *you* want?

At the end of the day what most of us seem to want is to be known, appreciated, loved. And in the storms of life, I think most of us want peace, safety, and security.

Have you ever been in a storm of life where you've made a bad choice or a series of bad choices?

You find yourself in the wrong room with the wrong people at the wrong time? In that kind of storm we can call out to Jesus using the lyrics of this old hymn written by Augustus Toplady in 1776,[2] "Please, Lord, *save from wrath and make me pure.*" And He'll be there. To save us from danger, from another mistake. All we need to do is take Jesus's hand and allow Him to lead us out of there— back to the east side of the park, perhaps. Jesus makes us pure all over again, as soon as we whimper, "I'm sorry."

Have you ever been in a storm where your heart is wounded?

Where you feel like your *tears (could) forever flow?* Jesus is with you in that storm too. He'll hold you, wipe your tears, and help you stand again. When no one else can, when nothing else will do it, *Thou must save, and Thou alone.*

Have you ever been in a storm when you felt helpless?

The airplane jerks and shakes, and you fear you're going down, but you can't fly a plane. Your child is actively pursuing harmful behavior, but you are incapable of stopping them. Your company is laying people off. You see it coming, but no matter how hard you work, your position will not exist in a few days. When there is not one thing you can do to change a bad situation, there is One who can rescue you. *Naked, come to Thee for dress; helpless look to Thee for grace.*

I don't think they meant to, but Def Leppard asked the question that only has one true answer.

What do you *want?*

The Bible tells us that God put eternity in our hearts, meaning our hearts will always be seeking, or wanting God, whether we understand that longing or not.

> He has made everything beautiful in its time. He has also set eternity in the human heart; yet no one can fathom what God has done from beginning to end. (Ecclesiastes 3:11)

We want the thing that satisfies our needs, cares for us in ways we could never ask for. We want the One who always recognizes us, sees us, protects us, and loves us, even in the deep, dark storms of life. What do we want? We want Jesus. Our safe place. Our cleft. He is the Rock of Ages.

Rock of Ages, cleft for me, let me hide myself in Thee.

This powerful hymn of desperation actually reminds me of the classic tune "Stand by Me" by Ben E. King.[3] Are you snapping your fingers yet? The singer of the song says that even when it's dark, even when he's frightened, even if the sky falls, and the mountains crumble, he won't be afraid. He won't cry, just as long as the one he's singing to (could it be God?) stands by his side.

Are your mountains crumbling? Does it feel like your sky is falling down? Are you caught in a storm and headed in the wrong direction? What do you want? What do you need protection from? Jesus is there. Standing by you. Always.

I don't know about you, but when I'm drenched and rattled, when I'm out of sorts and can't find my way, I want to sprint to my Rock. I long to hide myself in His cleft. I want Him to be the One standing by my side. And when I'm in His presence, whatever happened before doesn't bother me, the storms that rage outside can't harm me, whatever I was looking for I now find. I am safe, warm, dry, at home, and not alone. Jesus, the Rock of Ages. That's what I truly want. How about you?

CONTEMPLATE

God is good, a hiding place in tough times. (Nahum 1:7 MSG)

1. Can you remember a time you were in a life storm?

2. How has God been your Rock, a cleft or safe spot for you?

14

TURN YOUR EYES UPON JESUS

Helen H. Lemmel, 1922,
based on gospel tract,
"Focused," by Lilias Trotter

O soul, are you weary and troubled?
No light in the darkness you see?
There's a light for a look at the Savior,
And life more abundant and free!

> *Turn your eyes upon Jesus,*
> *Look full in His wonderful face,*
> *And the things of earth will grow*
> *strangely dim,*
> *In the light of His glory and grace.*

Through death into life everlasting
He passed, and we follow Him there;
Over us sin no more hath dominion—
For more than conquerors we are!

His Word shall not fail you—He promised;
Believe Him, and all will be well:
Then go to a world that is dying,
His perfect salvation to tell!

How Hymns Center Us

My father-in-law was unconscious, the rhythm of his machines thrummed through his dimly lit room at the Cleveland Clinic. Despite the somber atmosphere, Johnny Cash, the Big Bopper, and Elvis all sang their top hits through the speakers, rockabilly guitars strumming along to a toe-tapping beat. This is what Rick wanted. An upbeat soundtrack reminding us all of his gigantic, robust character as we took turns saying farewell. But even with the tunes, sorrow filled our hearts. We knew it was goodbye.

The first liver transplant hadn't worked. My father-in-law was on the list for a second one, but his body was weak. It was doubtful he could make it through another eight-hour surgery. I was driving our son Max to golf lessons when my husband called.

"I have to go to Cleveland." Brett's usually chipper voice sounded strained. "Dad's not doing well."

"I'm so sorry." I inhaled. "Of course you need to go—when?"

"I'm just going to pack and hit the road." Brett paused. "Is that okay?"

We were used to this back-and-forth conversation—as used to it as one can get—my husband not wanting to leave us, but wanting to be at his father's side, needing to depart at a moment's notice and without any definitive return date.

"Should we all go?" I asked, sensing something deeper in Brett's tone.

Silence.

I pulled into a gas station. If we were leaving for Cleveland, Max and I would need to head back home, call teachers and coaches, pack up.

"Yeah," my husband choked. "Yeah, if we can. I'd like you to all be with me."

Max and I turned around. We threw toothbrushes, teddy bears, and T-shirts into a giant suitcase and drove. Brett's car knew the five-hour route to the clinic on autopilot.

My husband was exhausted from the emotional strain of trying to be strong for all his family: me, the kids, his parents, and siblings. All the while Brett watched his powerful dad go through the rigmarole of hospitals, tubes, tanks, and tests—shrinking physically and emotionally throughout the process. My husband felt helpless. I felt helpless to help him.

What do you do when you're out of options? When you've made the calls, driven the roads, prayed the prayers, and you're at the end of yourself? I think that's the thing. There's nothing left for us to do. But we don't have to carry the load. We can turn our eyes to the One who never ends, who is always there, whose power is made perfect in our weakness (2 Corinthians 12:9). We can turn our eyes to Jesus.

The hymn "Turn Your Eyes upon Jesus," written by Helen H. Lemmel in 1922, is based on words from a gospel tract written by Lilias Trotter titled "Focused."[1] The lyrics remind us of what a comfort it is to lay our sorrows and troubles at Jesus's feet, so we don't have to bear them, so we can live freely.

O soul, are you weary and troubled? No light in the darkness you see? There's a light for a look at the Savior, and life more abundant and free!

The apostle Paul speaks to this coming to the end of ourselves. He had a "thorn in his side." Theologians argue as to what his "thorn" was, but everyone seems to agree Paul had an affliction, which made his life challenging.

> Three times I pleaded with the Lord to take it away from me. But he said to me, "My grace is sufficient for you, for my power is made perfect in weakness." Therefore I will boast all the more gladly about my weaknesses, so that Christ's power may rest on me. That is why, for Christ's sake, I delight in weaknesses, in insults, in hardships, in persecutions, in difficulties. For when I am weak, then I am strong. (2 Corinthians 12:8–10)

We identified with Paul. We'd pleaded with God to heal Rick. More than three times. But God answered that His power would be made perfect in our weakness. And although I'd be lying if I said I "delighted" in this hardship, I was grateful Jesus was by our side, and that He was strong in all the places we were weak.

So, I prayed fervently for my husband to feel Christ's peace, for my father-in-law to know the Lord, for my kiddos to understand what was going on, but at the same time not be frightened, for the love of Jesus to envelop my mother-in-law. These prayers, just looking to Him, talking to Him, were calming. Soothing. Keeping my eyes on Jesus was the only card I had in my hand. Thankfully, He beats trump and is higher than an ace every single time.

Turn your eyes upon Jesus, look full in His wonderful face.

I wanted my kids to understand that even though they would miss Papa dearly, there was still so much Jesus had in store for them. So I treated my kiddos to sweet, frothy strawberry-banana smoothies from the hospital cafeteria, walked them around the gorgeous grounds running our fingers through cool, trickling fountains, and explored the art displayed in the lobby ranging from a sculpture of a man built out of steel alphabet letters to a video installation of a colorful, spinning tree. I wanted them to sense Jesus's love—that even in loss He had wonderful things for them to experience. I believe Jesus wants this for us too. That in our darkest moments, He whispers, "Don't look at the darkness. Turn your eyes to Me. All those problems and pains will fade away if you fix your eyes on the life, the vibrancy I offer."

And the things of earth will grow strangely dim, in the light of His glory and grace.

Despite the delightful distractions with my kiddos, there came a time for me to enter the yellowish glow of my father-in-law's cramped hospital room with fifties favorites serenading me from the speakers. I choked out the words I wanted him to hear.

"Thank you for never treating me like an in-law—for loving me as if I was your own daughter. From the very first day you held out your arms, gave me bear hugs, asked me questions, lovingly teased me as if I'd always been part of the family—never an outsider stepping in. When I struggled with my dad, you reminded me what it felt like to be supported and accepted."

I didn't know if Rick could hear me or not. But I like to think he could. Tears leaked down my cheeks as I spoke in one soliloquy what I'd whispered to him in pieces over years. I wanted to tell my father-in-law how much I loved and appreciated him, but I believed Jesus wanted me to share more—how much He loved Rick. So I did.

Rick had a giant heart, but had never been much into faith. He was a self-made man born poor. He moved fourteen times by the time he was sixteen. Rick hustled, ground it out, took risks, and built his own company. Growing up, he hadn't been exposed to God, and as an adult, Rick never understood Jesus's role in his life. He attended church on Easter and Christmas because it was important to Brett's mom. Through tears and snot I told Rick that Jesus made him, loved him, always had and always would. I squeezed Rick's hand, kissed his cheek, and left the room.

His Word shall not fail you—He promised; believe Him, and all will be well.

Others took their turns. This was a time for true confessions, final wishes, words that weren't meant for an audience. But my husband shared one conversation he'd had with his dad while he was still conscious. Rick said to Brett, "I'm ready for Him. And He's ready for me."

Just typing that chokes me up.

In the end Rick was ready to be with God, and he finally understood that Jesus was ready and waiting for him.

Through death into life everlasting, He passed, and we follow Him there.

There are still days when I miss my father-in-law. When his deep, rolling laugh fills my ears. When I wish my mother-in-law didn't have to face life without him. When I would love for him to witness my daughter score a goal or my son recite his lines. But if we lost Rick so he could find Jesus? Then, wow. Yes! That changes everything. Then the ways of this world—wanting Rick to be here for us, for our comfort and happiness—do seem strangely dim, in the midst of the grace Christ offers.

I doubt I'll ever understand why some are healed and others not. But I am so grateful for a Savior who values spiritual healing above all else, who truly wants us *all* to be with Him, and who fights for every one of us 'till the end. I longed for Rick to be healed. But when I kept my eyes on Jesus, I realized Christ had an even more beautiful plan. Healing beyond my imagination.

Christ's power of salvation is made perfect in our human frailty. When we fix our eyes on Him, we begin to comprehend that His grace is sufficient. It's all we truly need.

CONTEMPLATE

Three times I pleaded with the Lord to take it away from me. But he said to me, "My grace is sufficient for you, for my power is made perfect in weakness." Therefore I will boast all the more gladly about my weaknesses, so that Christ's power may rest on me. That is why, for Christ's sake, I delight in weaknesses, in insults, in hardships, in persecutions, in difficulties. For when I am weak, then I am strong. (2 Corinthians 12:8–10)

1. Is there a "thorn" in your life right now that seems to be impeding you from moving forward?

2. Every time this issue comes up this week intentionally take a breath and picture Jesus—turn your eyes to Him. Keep track of

   • the instances where you feel out of control or at the end of your rope;

   • what you did to intentionally focus on Christ (read a Bible passage, say a prayer, utter His name, picture His face); and

   • how this process of focusing made you feel.

15

WERE YOU THERE?

African American spiritual,
first printed in 1899

Were you there when they crucified my Lord?
Were you there when they crucified my Lord?
Oh! Sometimes it causes me to tremble, tremble,
   tremble.
Were you there when they crucified my Lord?

Were you there when they nailed Him to the tree?
Were you there when they nailed Him to the tree?
Oh! Sometimes it causes me to tremble, tremble,
   tremble.
Were you there when they nailed Him to the tree?

Were you there when they laid Him in the tomb?
Were you there when they laid Him in the tomb?
Oh! Sometimes it causes me to tremble, tremble,
   tremble.
Were you there when they laid Him in the tomb?

Were you there when He rose up from the dead?
Were you there when He rose up from the dead?
Oh! Sometimes I feel like shouting, "Glory, glory,
    glory!"
Were you there when He rose up from the dead?

How Hymns Take Us to the Cross

I have cross necklaces, cross earrings, and a collection
of crosses from our travels including a beautiful bubbly blue stained-glass cross from the month we lived in
Lyon, France; a cross with thick, brightly colored, coarse
threads stitched in neat rows from a two-week stint our
family spent in the villages of Guatemala; and a smooth
porcelain tile with a glossy yellow-and-blue cross painted
on it from an anniversary trip to the Amalfi Coast of
southern Italy. I even have a simple black cross tattooed
on the inside of my left wrist. Do you have any crosses?
Where do you display them? What do you think about
when you see a cross?

As a Christian I know since Jesus died on the cross
on Calvary over two thousand years ago, I will experience eternal life. Our Savior's crucifixion led to our freedom. My entire life is changed, better, and fuller because
of what Jesus chose to do. My beautiful hand-crafted
crosses from around the world displayed on the wall
in our kitchen like a giant collage are a lovely reminder
of Jesus and His love—of what He offers, of what He's
given me. However, these gorgeous crosses and my lovely

silver cross pendant with a sweet little heart at the apex don't emphasize what took place that day when the King of kings was brutally executed like a criminal.

The torture Jesus endured is described in all four gospel accounts, Matthew 27, Mark 15, Luke 23, and John 19. I'll be the first to admit, blood and guts—not my thing. At all. I turn my head from anything slightly gory on the big screen and have zero interest in watching medical dramas. No *ER* or *Grey's Anatomy* for me. I can't stomach it. But to truly understand what Jesus did for us, I think it's important to take a peek at what happened on the cross. Stay with me, I'll try to make it brief. This is a truth we can't water down or avoid.

Here's the "Smith Notes" version of the crucifixion. In his award-winning book *A Case for Christ*, former legal editor of the Chicago Tribune, Lee Strobel interviews medical expert Dr. Alexander Metherell about crucifixion, about what Jesus endured that day for us.[1] Metherell describes the excruciating whipping and flogging that took place prior to Jesus being hung on the cross, which caused intense bruising and sliced Christ's flesh. Deep cuts, exposed muscles, and blood everywhere. Apparently many criminals died from this brutal torture without ever making it to the cross. But Jesus went the whole mile for us. He did not give up or give in despite the humiliation and crippling pain.

Next, nails were pounded through the nerves in Jesus's wrists and ankles. Jesus was hung in such a way that He couldn't breathe. Jesus needed to contort and twist His raw, torn up back against the rough wooden cross to catch gasps of breath. In the end, Jesus died of a heart attack when His human body could no longer endure all of the merciless punishment. He took His final breath.

Okay, our turn to catch our breath, because I don't know about you, but I'm feeling a little shaky—a bit trembly. If I'm faced with the choice of pain or no pain, I choose no pain. Every. Single. Time. I have birthed four babies and opted for an epidural (which numbed me from the waist down) for all four births.

Breathe in. Breathe out.

The flogging, the whipping, the dangling by iron nails—it's so much to take in. But it's what Jesus chose to do for us. And that's the crux of the spiritual "Were You There?"

Oh! Sometimes it causes me to tremble, tremble, tremble. Were you there when they crucified my Lord?

What would it have been like to be there that day? Imagine it's you sitting on the hill with a few other faithful women. Knowing Jesus changed your life. He called you by name, said you had worth, value, mattered. Even though most people at that time considered women property. Even though it was publicly known what you did, what condition you were in. Jesus still reached out to you. He was inclusive. His inner circle consisted of tax collectors, sinners, commoners. Yet there He hung, battered and bloody, and there was not a single thing you could do to stop it. Rushing to the cross, knocking down a guard, mouthing off to someone in charge. Those things would have gotten you killed. And Jesus would still be nailed there.

Were you there when they nailed Him to the tree?

One way of recalling this day is a Good Friday service. Have you attended one? Maybe with a darkened room illuminated by the pale light of candles. People are often asked to remain silent—a service of solemnness, to remember what Jesus endured. "Were You There?" is the perfect hymn to accompany the mood. In the flickering of candlelight, the heavy smell of wax, and the stillness of the sanctuary can you picture Jesus? Perfect Jesus, tears streaming down His face. Gasping for breath. The ultimate sacrifice for our sins. The definitive act of love.

Thankfully for the followers who saw Jesus laid in a tomb, this line, *Were you there when they laid Him in the tomb?*, isn't the end of the song or the end of the story. Which means it's also not the end of our story. But the disciples didn't know that yet.

All of the torture took place on Friday.

Saturday was a day of despair for those who loved Jesus. Hiding inside. Cowering. Fearing for their lives because they'd been seen hanging out with Jesus. And now that He'd been "taken care of," the officials decided it was time to go after the riffraff who followed Him. But the disciples were almost too sad to be scared. Was their hope completely gone?

Then Sunday happened. Who saw it coming? They should have. Because Jesus said He would rise on the third day. But it was confusing—difficult to get your mind around. Until now. Now the disciples (and we too) have a new reason to tremble. This time in amazement and joy.

Oh! Sometimes I feel like shouting glory, glory, glory. Were you there when He rose up from the dead?

Just like that there was an empty tomb! No man could have endured what Jesus went through. Historical and medical evidence prove He died.

His heart stopped beating.

His lungs stopped breathing.

But something incredible happened behind that stone—in that tomb. Jesus's heart caught its rhythm again. His lungs expanded. Jesus conquered death.

Recalling the first Good Friday hundreds of years ago in Jerusalem makes us tremble. Mosaic MSC sings in their modern song, "Tremble," that Jesus makes even the darkness tremble.[2] Jesus took all the sin, hate, and evil in the world—and made that darkness tremble. Then, and still today. Jesus conquered the grave for eternity. For you and for me. And this is what all the crosses in our lives represent.

Yes, crosses can be pretty. We might grab the cross around our neck when we recall miraculously coming to a safe stop as our wheels slid on the road or as we talk about an unexpected kindness someone extended. I tend to rub my cross tattoo when sharing how God has been working in my life, how one of my kids has found quality friends, or how the faith-based research my husband is doing at a public school has so far been blessed. Because great is our God! Crosses are a great reminder of who we are, Who we follow, but they are not to be taken lightly. What Jesus went through on the cross at Calvary was not light. When we take time to visualize what actually happened on the cross, we'll get a vivid illustration of whose we are and how unfathomable His love is for us.

It will make us tremble.

CONTEMPLATE

Then Pilate had Jesus flogged with a lead-tipped whip. (John 19:1 NLT)

There they nailed him to the cross. (John 19:18 NLT)

And since the tomb was close at hand, they laid Jesus there. (John 19:42 NLT)

While it was still dark, Mary Magdalene came to the tomb and found that the stone had been rolled away from the entrance. (John 20:1 NLT)

1. Do you own any crosses? What do you think of when you see them?

2. Read John 19:1–20:10. What part of the crucifixion sticks out the most to you?

3. When reflecting on "Were You There?," which part makes you tremble?

4. How will you stay focused on what Christ did for you on the cross throughout the week?

16

NOTHING
BUT THE BLOOD

Robert Lowry, 1876

What can wash away my sin?
Nothing but the blood of Jesus.
What can make me whole again?
Nothing but the blood of Jesus.

> *Oh! precious is the flow*
> *That makes me white as snow;*
> *No other fount I know,*
> *Nothing but the blood of Jesus.*

For my pardon, this I see:
Nothing but the blood of Jesus.
For my cleansing, this my plea:
Nothing but the blood of Jesus.

Nothing can for sin atone:
Nothing but the blood of Jesus.

Naught of good that I have done:
Nothing but the blood of Jesus.

This is all my hope and peace:
Nothing but the blood of Jesus.
This is all my righteousness:
Nothing but the blood of Jesus.

Now by this I'll overcome—
Nothing but the blood of Jesus.
Now by this I'll reach my home—
Nothing but the blood of Jesus.

Glory! Glory! This I sing—
Nothing but the blood of Jesus.
All my praise for this I bring—
Nothing but the blood of Jesus.

How Hymns Renew Us

Recently a deer jumped in front of my husband's car taking his passenger side mirror with it as it leapt into the woods. We opted not to replace it, so a mangled metal stump is all that remains. The odometer reads over 150,000 miles. Let's just say his car isn't fancy. However, despite the wear and tear, my husband's car is considered a "luxury brand" requiring high-octane fuel—the expensive kind. Believe me, we've attempted filling up with middle grade gas, but his car protests—pinging and chirping as it burns its way through that entire tank of fuel. Yes, his car still runs, goes, moves on the cheaper gasoline, but it isn't what it truly requires or needs to run at its optimum efficiency. As soon as we refill it with the "good stuff," his car hums and purrs like a kitten lapping a saucer of cream.

My youngest has eczema, and in the winter his skin is a mess. He gets all red, splotchy, and itchy, resembling a walking, talking rash. We've tried every lotion and cream to hydrate his ultra-dry skin. And they help some. But when his eczema flares, he needs to use his prescription hydrocortisone. If he diligently rubs the thick, white cream onto his itchy patches of skin several days in a row, his eczema clears up. Every time. The other lotions relieve some redness and itch, but they don't make it go away. Only the medicated cream prescribed by his allergist can heal.

I'm guilty of settling for serviceable, when there's really a better way, an ideal solution—whether that's cheaper gas or more convenient cream. You?

Sometimes we try to get away with what seems like the easier alternative. Sometimes we honestly don't know the solution, so we dabble with trial and error attempting to solve our problems. And this is okay when we're out of trash bags, and reuse a bag from Old Navy to gather our garbage. But when it comes to filling that longing, that emptiness inside of us, making up for where we've messed up—there's only one thing that truly works.

A simple hymn first sung at a camp in Ocean Grove, New Jersey, in 1876,[1] "Nothing but the Blood" reminds us of our one true solution.

What can make me whole again? Nothing but the blood of Jesus.

But I often go for the metaphorical cheaper gas or the reused bag. I want to please people, to "do the right thing" for people to think the best of me, and I want to do it now. And so I attempt to be perfect when I'm actually closer to cheap gas or generic lotion.

Like Easter this year. I'm big into holidays and wanted this one to be a day filled with love, memories, traditions, and infused with faith for family and our friends from church we'd invited over for brunch. I planned, shopped, cooked, and hard-boiled eggs. But the egg dye tablets plus the allotted amount of vinegar and room temperature water only filled one centimeter of the cups with vibrant colors—not nearly enough to submerge an egg. I followed the directions. I thought. But something was definitely not working. I forgot to buy the ranch dressing at the store, and had to send my husband back, even though I wanted to make his life easier. Plus, the coffee cake was still gooey on top even though it should have been done baking. I got frustrated and frazzled, and felt like a failure . . . until I remembered what makes a really excellent Easter.

Jesus dying on the cross to save sinners like me, like you, and then rising from the grave, offering us everlasting life.

How glorious Easter is, as it turns out, has nothing to do with me, my effort, my performance, how well I did or did not please people, but everything to do with Jesus.

Naught of good that I have done: nothing but the blood of Jesus.

And yes, Easter makes for an easy example, but that's why I'm using it. If I can lose perspective on what matters on the day that most defines me as a Christian, you can imagine what a mess I am on regular days.

I raise my voice at my teenage daughter because her laundry is sitting out. But she is overloaded with homework, and her friend with mental health issues is heavy on her mind. My comment deflates my beautiful girl. I feel awful, guilty, and later run some M&M's up to her room and put away that laundry for her when she's not looking. Which are nice things to do. But they aren't saying, "I'm sorry." They're not going to Jesus for help. And they're not remembering that my value as a mama is not based on always saying the right thing. My mom clout comes from the fact that Jesus allowed me to have these kiddos. And because He bought me with the price of His blood, I am forgiven for not realizing how much pressure my girl was under and pardoned for all my other faux pas, as well.

For my pardon, this I see: nothing but the blood of Jesus.

Yes, I should keep trying to be a good mom. I should keep attempting to write well, to convey Christ's love to those who stumble across my words. But some days I feel like I'm the one stumbling as I write. We are called to love the people God has put in front of us, to perform the tasks He has assigned us, and to do them to the best of our ability.

But no coffee cake (not even one with a perfect brown sugar swirl and sweet, creamy icing dripping along the edges) or peace offering of putting away clothes (no matter how giant the pile) can make us whole. Only blood can purify. That's always been the case.

People aren't perfect.

We mess up. Which is sin.

God is perfect, and our sin and His holiness repel each other like opposing ends of a magnet. But God wants to be with us, so He figured out a way to make that happen. Blood, which symbolizes life, can clean up our sin, so God can get close to us.

> For without the shedding of blood, there is no forgiveness. (Hebrews 9:22 NLT)

In Genesis 22, God tells Abraham to go to the land of Moriah to offer a blood sacrifice. In Exodus 12, God instructs Moses to have the Israelites spread lamb's blood over their front doors so they could escape death. In 2 Samuel 6, King David sacrifices the blood of a bull and a fattened calf as he brings the ark of the covenant into the city. In 2 Chronicles 29, King Hezekiah reopens the temple. First, Hezekiah kills seven bulls, seven rams, seven male lambs, and seven male goats—using their blood as a way to "clean" the temple after it had been rejected and defiled by the previous king. Then all the people came and sacrificed seventy bulls, one hundred rams, and two hundred male lambs. The animals designated as sacrifices altogether included six hundred bulls and three thousand sheep and goats! Whew. That's so many animals. So much blood. I could go on and on list-ing more examples of blood sacrifice. But those days are over, so let's not dwell on them.

Jesus came once and for all to do away with that old system, to be the perfect, final blood sacrifice, cleans-ing us, purifying us, making us worthy, loveable, and accepted forever. Nothing else can do it. Everything else is a cheap substitute, a quick fix that won't really do the job. But what Jesus did on the cross for us. *Sigh*. So pre-cious. We are forever more soaked in His forgiveness and love.

Oh! precious is the flow that makes me white as snow; no other fount I know, nothing but the blood of Jesus.

And so, we can stop itching and scratching, feeling uncomfortable about how we fall short. We are forever soothed by the balm of Jesus pouring out His blood—His life for us. We can stop trying to run on low-octane fuel. We can move through our days with maximum efficiency because we have an endless fount of love and forgiveness to propel us forward.

This is all my hope and peace: nothing but the blood of Jesus.

CONTEMPLATE

Now that we are set right with God by means of this sacrificial death, the consummate blood sacrifice, there is no longer a question of being at odds with God in any way. If, when we were at our worst, we were put on friendly terms with God by the sacrificial death of his Son, now that we're at our best, just think of how our lives will expand and deepen by means of his resurrection life! (Romans 5:9–10 MSG)

1. Can you think of a time you tried to make up for a mistake you made by yourself? How did it turn out?

2. How does it make you feel knowing "there is no longer a question of being at odds with God in any way" (Romans 5:9)?

17

HOLY, HOLY, HOLY

Reginald Heber, 1826,
written for Trinity Sunday

Holy, holy, holy! Lord God Almighty!
Early in the morning our song shall rise to thee.
Holy, holy, holy! Merciful and mighty!
God in three persons, blessed Trinity!

Holy, holy, holy! All the saints adore thee,
Casting down their golden crowns around the
    glassy sea;
Cherubim and seraphim falling down before thee,
Which wert, and art, and evermore shalt be.

Holy, holy, holy! Though the darkness hide thee,
Though the eye of sinful man thy glory may not
    see,
Only thou art holy; there is none beside thee,
Perfect in power, in love, and purity.

Holy, holy, holy! Lord God Almighty!
All thy works shall praise thy name in earth and
    sky and sea.
Holy, holy, holy! Merciful and mighty!
God in three persons, blessed Trinity.

How Hymns Help Us Worship

The "Three in One" is a juggling trick where three balls
are thrown and caught all by the same hand.[1] Three in
One is the name of a Chinese restaurant in Colonia, New
Jersey. Three-in-one has also become a bit of a catch
phrase for handy gadgets. Much like the Thneeds knitted
by the Once-ler in Dr. Seuss's *The Lorax*, a three-in-one is
the thing touted as something "which everyone, EVERY-
ONE, *EVERYONE* needs."[2] There are 122 "3-in-1"
items listed for sale on QVC today ranging from coffee
makers, hampers, potato peelers, motor oils, to saws.[3]
Maybe because we're all trying to get so much done in
so little time. Maybe because Americans are so stressed,
more so now than ever.[4] And if we could just have something do three things for us, *whew*, that would be a relief.
But long before there were 3-in-1 pressure cookers and
winter boots, our God was the original 3-in-1: the Father,
the Son, and the Holy Spirit.

We seem to have no problem conceptualizing that we
could use one car seat to hold a tiny infant facing back-
ward on her way home from the hospital, the same seat a
few months later when she's big enough to face forward,

and a few years later still be using it, when she no longer requires all of the side padding but still needs a "boost" to make her the right height for a normal seat belt to fit correctly. Yet, we as humans struggle with the concept of a Holy Trinity—Father, Son, and Holy Spirit, each distinct, yet one. And because it's a who rather than a what, it's even more complicated. Whether or not we can wrap our brains around this concept, we *can* focus on the fact that God is better than anything you'll ever find on QVC or Amazon.

He's the ultimate. He doesn't just get the job done, or three of the jobs done; He gets them all done, perfectly. God is loving, fair, just, strong, powerful, pure, kind, capable, good, worthy, forgiving, and understanding, just to name a few of His attributes. God is also holy.

In the Bible, when words are repeated, it's often for emphasis. I've always wondered if the hymn "Holy, Holy, Holy" was giving one "holy" to each member of the Trinity, or if it was just declaring that God deserves a trio of "holies" because He's just that awesome. And even though we know this gorgeous hymn was written by songwriter Reginald Heber specifically to praise the Holy Trinity, even with the intent to have it sung on "Trinity Sunday" (which falls eight weeks after Easter on a liturgical calendar),[5] we don't know how he was handing out those three holies. But no matter how the triad of holies was intended, this song makes me want to drop to my knees.

The second verse describes everyone else who's falling down at Jesus's feet, and I don't want to do it because they're doing it, but because when I look at the powerful, holy beings who deem Jesus worthy and say He's the holy one, then wow, I think I better let how purely our Lord is the epitome of holy sink in deep. This verse starts with: *Holy, holy, holy! All the saints adore Thee, casting down their golden crowns around the glassy sea.*

It says *all* the saints. Not some of them. And these saints, who have lived pretty amazing lives and loved well, they're quick to say about themselves, about their accomplishments, "Whatever," and throw down their crowns completely letting go of them, discarding them, declaring that next to Jesus, none of their achievements matter. So, that deal we closed last week? The savory, cheesy lasagna we're kind of famous for? All the money we raised for the fundraiser? Not so impressive after all. Maybe we should quit bragging about our accomplishments, and lay those aside. Maybe we should forget about them altogether so we can better focus on Jesus and His pure loveliness—His holiness.

And if the whole gathering of saints isn't enough to convince us, next come the angels: *cherubim and seraphim falling down before Thee.* The whole thing is an image straight out of the book of Revelation, chapter 4. Even the part about the angels singing these words to God, *which wert, and art, and evermore shalt be.* Because God was there before anything else. He created every single thing. And He's here now. *Emmanuel,* which means "God with us." And He will be with us for all the days to come.

The Bible speaks of this from Genesis when God forms the heavens and earth, then walks around the garden with Adam and Eve, to the gospels of Matthew, Mark, Luke, and John where Jesus incarnate walks the earth, to Revelation when we get to hang out with Him for eternity, doing what the saints and angels are doing—worshiping Him. Phillips, Craig, and Dean feature this in their number one hit, "Revelation Song," a modern hymn based on this same text, in which we sing to God that He is our everything, and we will adore Him.[6]

Which brings us back to why we're worshiping Jesus in the first place, because *there is none beside Thee*. He is Everything—everything that matters, everything that truly satisfies, that truly fulfills our needs. He's *perfect in power, in love, and purity*. And really, when we focus on the attributes of Jesus, of who He truly is, of what He does for us, what He did for us on the cross, how He loves us. *Wow!* It's way more amazing than Ginsu knives.

I am blown away. And everything I was worried about accomplishing, getting to, taking care of dissolves. Because *there is none beside Thee*.

Since Jesus is my King, why would I worry about dropping sales numbers on Amazon or fret over how I'm going to manage the awkward situation of my divorced parents both wanting to attend my child's graduation. God's in such perfect control, no one can top what He's got going on. When we turn this all over to Him, we still need to be active and engage, but we do *not* need to worry or think it's up to us. And because of His goodness, His aptitude in all things, we can start each day praising Him. *Early in the morning our song shall rise to Thee.* We can start each day fresh and reassured that our God is *Holy, holy, holy*! He is *merciful.* And our Lord is *mighty.*

These definitions apply to God the Father, who created us, who cradles us when we're weak, confused, broken, sad, and at the end of our ropes. They apply to Jesus, His Son, who lived in human form to experience our every relief, grief, despair, and triumph. Who died on the cross taking the punishment for our sins. These truths apply to the Holy Spirit, the Helper, whom Jesus sent to whisper to us and direct us every step of our daily existence. We may or may not understand how God can be three-in-one and one-in-three, but we can accept that His goodness, His authority, the way He loves, leads, and saves us, is manifested in a multifaceted loving trio. And this is a purely fantastic, brilliant, and holy thing. *God in three persons, blessed Trinity.*

CONTEMPLATE

Day and night they never stop saying: "'Holy, holy, holy is the Lord God Almighty,' who was, and is, and is to come." (Revelation 4:8)

1. Read Revelation chapter 4 (don't worry, it's super short). Close your eyes and imagine the scene of everyone bowing down and worshiping Jesus. Jot down any thoughts, words, or ideas that come to mind.

2. How can you focus on God's holiness this week?

18

THE LORD'S PRAYER

Jesus
Matthew 6:9–13 (KJV)

Our Father which art in heaven,
    Hallowed be thy name.
Thy kingdom come,
    Thy will be done in earth,
    as it is in heaven.
Give us this day our daily bread.
And forgive us our debts,
    as we forgive our debtors.
And lead us not into temptation,
    but deliver us from evil:
    For thine is the kingdom,
    and the power,
    and the glory,
    for ever. Amen.

How Hymns Help Us Pray

Christians, Jews, Muslims, and Hindus all do it.

Pray.

Growing up, our family gathered around our faux wood Formica table and prayed before passing the meatloaf covered in tangy, red sauce, "God is great. God is good. Let us thank Him for our food." Later, cozied up in soft-flannel pajamas we recited, "Now I lay me down to sleep." These were legitimate prayers, but they were more like sounds I said to a beat of a metronome than conversations with God.

So what's the difference between Christian prayer and the prayers of other world religions? How can the rote words of our childhood develop into something more meaningful? If we haven't been big on prayer before, how do we start?

We could Google "how to pray" or ask our friends— and we might get some pretty good answers, but how about going straight to the source?

Jesus showed Christians what their prayers should sound and look like. Jesus modeled a variety of prayers, depending on the situation. He went off by himself to pray (Mark 1:35), prayed over meals (Matthew 14:19), asked God to forgive people (Luke 23:34), and begged God for a change in plans and for God's will, both in one breath (Luke 22:42). Jesus showed us praying, talking to God, is a personal thing. A conversation. And can vary depending on the day or situation.

In the famous Sermon on the Mount, Jesus taught His followers about love, food, clothing, worries, payments, poverty, and so much more. Jesus also taught His disciples the basics of prayer. The Lord's Prayer, or as some traditions refer to it, the Our Father, is the prayer Jesus used as a model to illustrate what a "typical" prayer should look like. This doesn't mean every time we pray, we need to use these exact words. But it does mean this prayer has the elements Jesus wanted us to use in our prayers. It provides the perfect framework. The verses from Matthew 6:9–13 are also the lyrics to the hymn by the same name, "The Lord's Prayer."

Maybe "The Lord's Prayer" is another prayer or song you know by rote. You may have repeated it on Sundays growing up or sang it straight out of the hymnal—patent leather shoes too tight on your feet, wondering how many verses you would sing before the pastor dismissed you and you could rush to grab a sticky, sweet glazed donut from the fellowship hall.

Sometimes the things that are so familiar to us fall flat. Sometimes it's of value to look at them anew. If this is how Jesus wants us to pray, I don't want to gloss over it. I want to know what He meant.

Jesus begins by glorifying God, worshiping Him, acknowledging how powerful and magnificent God is. When we start prayer this way, it frames our conversation. It gets us away from who we hope God might be or who we think He should be or who we fear He could be, and straight to who He actually is—glorious. I love this translation, "Our Father, dwelling in the heavenly realms, may the glory of your name be the center on which our lives turn" (Matthew 6:9 TPT).

Yes! May everything I do and say rotate around the fact that God is in control, and He is so very good. Thank you, God, for that! When we fully realize this, then the things we're worried about seem less of a big deal because goodness is in control. When we start our prayers here, our requests tend to shift.

Instead of begging, "God please help me and my child not argue over this." I am reminded God is good. That He created my child in His image, and therefore my child is good. My prayer swings to something like this, "God, thank you for my child, and for your Son, Jesus. Please help me see all my kids through your eyes. Please help me love and listen to them well."

Did you notice the change? All because I first remembered who God is.

The hymn continues, *Give us this day our daily bread.* Living in the Western world there aren't many days when I'm concerned if I'll get a slice of bread. In fact, with two gluten-free boys, we don't eat much bread in our house. But the intent is sound. Whatever we need today, we can ask God to provide. We can say, "God, I believe you will give me everything I need today—the food to fill my belly, the words to speak during my presentation, and the ability to bite my tongue when I disagree with my husband over something silly, because arguing over what we had for dessert last Thanksgiving is pointless."

Everything we need today, God provides.

The next line of the prayer varies depending on your church, but the hymn goes like this: *And forgive us our debts, as we forgive our debtors.* No matter how you've learned it (trespasses or debts) Jesus wants us to ask for forgiveness for anything we've done wrong.

This puts us in a position of humility before we try to begrudgingly forgive someone else. It also reconciles us with God. We can pray something like, "God, I'm a mess. I'm impatient. I judge other people for their political views, how much TV they watch, or let their kids watch (or fill in the blank with your pet peeve). I didn't listen well to my friend because I was distracted. I snapped at my mother-in-law because of PMS, but still I shouldn't have snapped, and okay, I'll call her tonight and apologize."

Clearly, God is God and knows our mistakes. He doesn't need us to point them out. But God loves it when we come to Him. And when we spill our shortcomings to Jesus, we're relieved of the burden of our sins. We experience the liberation of His grace washing over us. In this sweet spot of Jesus's forgiveness, we're poised perfectly to extend grace to anyone who has wronged, owes, or "trespassed" against us.

By now in this hymn-prayer we should be feeling better inside—more aware of God's authority and grace. Reassured that what we need will be provided. We've been able to unload some guilt or regret, and turned the page on some resentment or anger.

And then as we're feeling refreshed, Jesus prays, *And lead us not into temptation, but deliver us from evil.*

He's telling us to flat out ask God for protection from messing up again and from any evil that might come our way. So if we know we're more tempted to gossip around "those people," we could pray, "Lord, please help me find another seat, get assigned another group, or be placed on a different committee." If we know we get snippy around "Larry" at work who rubs us the wrong way, then we can proactively pray, "God please help me see him as your creation. Help me find ways to reply with positive comments or remain silent when he makes *those* remarks." And if there's something truly evil pressing on us, Jesus instructs us to beg, "Please, oh please, God, keep my family and me safe from this horrible thing."

Jesus walks the disciples (and us) through a rock-solid prayer, then for the grand finale of the hymn He declares, *For Thine is the kingdom, and the power, and glory, for ever.* It doesn't matter if you speak it or sing it; this last line takes us right back to where we belong, at the foot of the throne, grateful for a King so worthy of our praise.

Suddenly all the thoughts and prayers that twisted through my brain, the friend who feels empty since her kids moved out, the uncle with upcoming surgery, the acquaintance struggling to pay his bills, the gal from Bible study trying to sell her house, my upcoming travels . . . all these things are put in their place—God's trustworthy hands.

The hymn reminds us that our Father is in heaven. He is good, large, and in charge. We should have no concerns about how He's tending the kingdom. Our daily bread? Our friend's and family's daily bread, health, bills, safety?

Jesus provides what we need—what they need. Even if we're frustrated with ourselves, we are washed clean in forgiveness because of Jesus's sacrifice. And because we're forgiven for all our garbage, it's easier to forgive others if they've hurt us. Our sweet Savior keeps us from evil, guards us from harm. Does this song make you feel at peace? Empowered? Grateful? It makes me feel all of the above, centered, and ready to face the day or night ahead.

I am in awe of our God, of Our Father who art in heaven. Hallowed be His name.

CONTEMPLATE

This, then, is how you should pray:
"Our Father in heaven,
hallowed be your name,
your kingdom come,
your will be done,
    on earth as it is in heaven.
Give us today our daily bread.
And forgive us our debts,
    as we also have forgiven our debtors.
And lead us not into temptation,
    but deliver us from the evil one."
(Matthew 6:9–13)

1. Do you have a go-to way you pray? Describe it here.

2. Do you follow the model Jesus taught us to pray? Praising Him, trusting Him, talking to Him about

your daily needs, asking forgiveness, forgiving others, asking for protection, and then praising Him again? If not, which parts do you usually leave out / hope to work on? Commit to using The Lord's Prayer as a framework for your prayers this week.

19

HE'S GOT THE WHOLE WORLD IN HIS HANDS

African American spiritual,
first published in 1927
Some sources point to Master Sergeant Obie
Edwin Philpot as the author[1]

He's got the whole world in His hands
He's got the whole world in His hands
He's got the whole world in His hands
He's got the whole world in His hands

He's got the little tiny baby in His hands
He's got the little tiny baby in His hands
He's got the little tiny baby in His hands
He's got the whole world in His hands

He's got you and me, brother, in His hands
He's got you and me, brother, in His hands
He's got you and me, brother, in His hands
He's got the whole world in His hands

He's got you and me, sister, in His hands
He's got you and me, sister, in His hands
He's got you and me, sister, in His hands
He's got the whole world in His hands

He's got everybody here in His hands
He's got everybody here in His hands
He's got everybody here in His hands
He's got the whole world in His hands

He's got the wind and the rain in His hands
He's got the wind and the rain in His hands
He's got the wind and the rain in His hands
He's got the whole world in His hands

He's got the sun and the moon in His hands
He's got the sun and the moon in His hands
He's got the sun and the moon in His hands
He's got the whole world in His hands

How Hymns Help Us Love

"This is my daughter, Sara," Faireh* said. "It's the only picture I have of her, but I want you to have it. Happy birthday." He handed my daughter, Maddie, the priceless square—the photo he had of his little girl he wouldn't see for another year and a half when he would finally return home to Afghanistan.

Part of a program for graduate students from Afghanistan studying in Ohio included homestays so the students

---

*This name has been changed to protect the individual's privacy.

could experience a day in the life of an American family. Faireh stayed at our house. In Afghanistan, Faireh is a medical doctor, husband, and father. In the United States, he's a student, living alone, and often glanced at sideways because of his accent and Middle Eastern features. The night he stayed with us was our daughter Maddie's birthday. Through conversation, we discovered it was also his daughter Sara's birthday! Faireh graciously apologized for not having a gift for our daughter.

How could he have one? How could he have known?

He tapped his pockets as if looking for a gift to magically appear, and then smiled, nodded, and pulled out a photo of his little girl.

Maddie tried to give it back to Faireh. We tried to explain to him this wasn't necessary. But to Faireh it was necessary. It was important to him to honor our daughter with something of value—and this was the most valuable thing he had.

The world got a little smaller for us that evening. Stereotypes about men from Afghanistan at a time when our nation has troops in their country were shattered, and replaced with images of a caring father. Our image of a man from Afghanistan is now of Faireh, who insisted on cooking a flavorful dinner of crispy rice topped with chicken in a fragrant sauce for our family—even though he was supposed to be the guest in our home. Now when I hear about Afghanistan in the news, I think of Faireh—a Middle Eastern man who gave away a piece of his heart to our daughter, who had a little girl with the same birthday as our little girl. The refrain of the African American spiritual "He's Got the Whole World in His Hands" plays in my mind.

When I was little, I loved this song. I'd nudge my brother, Jim, at the *He's got you and me, brother* line because I looked up to him so much. I'm pretty sure Jim viewed me as his pesky, younger sister. Jim is four years older. He was always leaps ahead of me in grades, height, knowledge, how late he could stay up, and more. But during this song, we were in the same place at the same time—in God's hands, and I liked the sound of that.

It's one thing to belt out, *He's got the wind and the rain in his hands*, in elementary school. It's another thing for us adults with opinions, biases, and experiences to truly consider sitting in God's hands with everyone else. Because there are some people we don't really want to be that close to, consider ourselves in the same boat, or hands as. Not that we get to decide who God does and doesn't love, but some days we'd like to, wouldn't we?

This hymn was passed down orally from person to person, meaning the verses and even the tune may change a bit depending on who you hear it from.[2] It also means you can feel free to change the lines and insert all kinds of folks in God's hands—that's the point after all, that we all belong in there together. Because of our friend Faireh, I'm comfortable singing this line, *He's got Americans and Afghanis in His hands*. But without knowing him, rubbing shoulders with someone from Afghanistan, a country on the other side of the world, with political tension, who speaks a different language, practices a different religion? That might be more challenging.

So let's start with an easy one. *He's got coffee and tea drinkers in his hands.* Hard to argue God loves us no matter what kind of warm beverage we pour in our mugs. Let's stay at home for this next one—keep it simple: *He's got the Democrats and Republicans in his hands.* Oh . . . was that one harder? Maybe not so simple. No matter which side of the ballot you vote, God loves you and the people who vote differently than you. He does because He made you, and He made them too.

Now you try—consider a group of people who think differently than you do, can you insert them and you in the same line of this song? Do you want to be in God's hands with them? Can you accept that God loves you and them? And if you sing this song, does it open your eyes, help you view others in a new light?

Because God loves *all* of us. The song says *the whole world*, and that includes your strange neighbor, the woman on your tennis team who rambles about her problems nonstop, your cousin who never disciplines her kids, and her kids who tried to flush a washcloth down your toilet the last time they visited. The other church or denomination, the one you left, God still has them in His hands. The boss who fired you, the frenemy who gossiped about you, the one who lied to you . . . It's so hard to believe or understand, but God has them *all* in His hands.

As Bob Goff says in *Everybody Always*, "If I really want to 'meet Jesus,' then I have to get a lot closer to the people He created. All of them, not just some of them."[3]

And when we question this, how could Jesus love them—the stinky, creepy, guy on the corner screaming curses, the opinionated, bossy woman who makes everyone feel small, the people who are so obviously different from us? We're called to remember, God loves us. And guess what? We have all let someone down, told lies, hidden secrets, put ourselves first, blurted out words we regret. And no matter how we feel about ourselves, no matter how much we question our abilities or endurance or size, Jesus loves us. And if He loves us, it makes sense that He also loves everyone else, no matter what they say, believe, or look like.

The apostle Paul lets us in on what he calls "the mystery."

> The mystery is that people who have never heard of God and those who have heard of him all their lives (what I've been calling outsiders and insiders) stand on the same ground before God. They get the same offer, same help, same promises in Christ Jesus. The Message is accessible and welcoming to everyone, across the board. (Ephesians 3:6 MSG)

Everyone. Across the board. We all stand on the same ground before God. What a relief! We stand on the same ground as the gal who looks like she has it all together, and the one who looks like a hot mess, and everyone in between. We stand on the same ground as our pastor and Beth Moore and whoever your favorite Bible study teacher is. We stand on the same ground as the other moms cheering at the games and the people we serve and the people who serve us.

And that ground is gorgeous ground. It's a place offering freedom and love. And it's accessible to everyone. The whole world. That's who God holds lovingly in His hands. Even *you and me, sister*!

CONTEMPLATE

The mystery is that people who have never heard of God and those who have heard of him all their lives (what I've been calling outsiders and insiders) stand on the same ground before God. They get the same offer, same help, same promises in Christ Jesus. The Message is accessible and welcoming to everyone, across the board. (Ephesians 3:6 MSG)

1. Name a group of people you struggle to love.

2. Name a specific person you struggle to love.

3. Write out a prayer thanking Jesus for loving you. Ask Him to help you love the ones you've mentioned above, to see them as His children, to embrace the idea of being nestled in His hands with them.

20

GIVE ME JESUS

African American spiritual, date unknown

In the morning, when I rise,
In the morning, when I rise,
In the morning, when I rise,
Give me Jesus.

> *Give me Jesus,*
> *Give me Jesus,*
> *You may have all this world,*
> *Give me Jesus.*

Dark midnight was my cry,
Dark midnight was my cry,
Dark midnight was my cry,
Give me Jesus.

Just about the break of day,
Just about the break of day,
Just about the break of day,
Give me Jesus.

When I am alone,
When I am alone,
Oh, when I am alone,
Give me Jesus.

Oh, when I come to die,
Oh, when I come to die,
Oh, when I come to die,
Give me Jesus.

And when I want to sing,
And when I want to sing,
And when I want to sing,
Give me Jesus.

Give me Jesus,
Give me Jesus,
You can have all this world,
You can have all this world,
You can have all this world,
Give me Jesus.

How Hymns Root Us

What's the first thing you think of when your alarm buzzes? That gorgeous, silky cyan scarf you're planning on wearing? If you have any sweet, ripe strawberries left for breakfast? Your to-do list? Finances? Family? The weather? The snooze button?

What's the last thought in your head as you nestle under your soft covers at night?

What you accomplished today? The deal you made? The dollars in or out of your account? What you still need to get done tomorrow? The caramel macchiato you're going to drink in the morning? How soon you'll be able to get it? Are you wriggling around trying to get comfortable because you have a sore knee or constant headaches? Or maybe it's not your body that hurts but your heart because of what someone said or didn't say—someone you were counting on. And that ache fills your thoughts when your head hits the pillow.

King Solomon shouldn't have had anything to worry about when he woke up or when he went to sleep. He was the wisest king to ever rule Israel, had lavish mansions, breathtaking gardens, wealth beyond compare. I won't even go into his wives and kids, but let's just say he wasn't lonely. Solomon didn't have any financial issues, or anyone he had to beat out for his position or office. If he needed something done, Solomon could send a slave, soldier, or staff member to take care of it. I promise, he never worried about what dinner would be because his chefs would put every contestant on the TV series *Chopped* to shame. And yet, Solomon begins the book of Ecclesiastes with, "Everything is meaningless . . . completely meaningless" (Ecclesiastes 1:2 NLT).

What? This guy had it all. No worries. As in zero.

Right?

Wrong. Because by having "everything" the world claims will make us happy, King Solomon learned those things didn't actually bring joy. Didn't bring peace. Didn't bring contentment. Only one thing does. Jesus.

And so, Solomon wraps up his dissertation with such lines as these: "Honor [your Creator] in your youth . . . Remember him before the light of the sun, moon, and stars is dim . . . Remember him before you become fearful of falling and worry about danger . . . Remember him before you near the grave . . . [And] yes, remember your Creator now while you are young" (Ecclesiastes 12:1, 2, 5–6 NLT). Basically, if you truly want to find meaning and joy in your life . . . remember God. All the time.

The old anonymously written spiritual "Give Me Jesus" sums up King Solomon's thoughts: *You can have all this world.* Just *give me Jesus.*

What if our first and last thoughts of each day were Jesus? About what He did for us, how much He loves us, how all the little details aren't worth worrying about because God's a BIG-picture kind of guy, like the biggest picture. And He's working out every single detail that has ever occurred in your life (and everyone else's) into one giant, gorgeous, glorious jigsaw puzzle.

> We know that for those who love God all things work together for good, for those who are called according to his purpose. (Romans 8:28 ESV)

If we lived with our minds more focused on Jesus and less on this world, we'd be a lot less stressed, have fewer headaches, laugh more, sleep better.

The first time I heard "Give Me Jesus" was just a few years ago. My musician friend Holly Starr was leading worship at our church. That morning my mind swirled with the stress of the upcoming week—so many things needed tending. Not nearly enough hours to get half of them done. A phone call I'd rather not have to make was looming. The person on the other side of the call seemed to manipulate every conversation we had and consistently made me feel inadequate. Just thinking about the call made my stomach churn. I was having my frequent inner argument about how to balance hours between ministry and mommy-ing. Was it neglecting God's call for me to be a wife and mom if I accepted a new project I'd been offered? Was I disregarding God's call for me to teach His people if I said no? All this tossed inside me.

And then Holly sang this lyric: *You can have all this world. Give me Jesus.*

My knees buckled.

Yes, I thought, you (whoever the proverbial *you* is) can have all this world. I don't want it—the stress, pain, concerns, heartache, tension.

Do you?

No, thanks. Give me Jesus!

Because here's the thing. Solomon was right. The things of this world are meaningless. Those worries about how to spend our time? If we talk to God and trust Him for guidance, He'll show us what to do and when to do it. He'll provide us opportunities to use our gifts for Him. And the stress that creeps up our necks when calculating the number of hours it'll take to accomplish the things on our lists; and the way we feel when we hear that intimidating person's voice; and the incompleteness we experience when we get the clothes in the washer, and then the dryer, but never get them folded; when baby carrots—you know the ones that come peeled, and ready to eat—are the "side dish" we're serving for dinner—again; when we notice the light bulb is burned out in the hallway but simply don't have time to change it (not to mention we probably don't have the right size bulb, which would require a trip to the store, and if we don't have time to change the bulb, we don't have time to run an errand)—all of that incompleteness evaporates with one phrase—*You can have all this world. Give me Jesus!*

Seriously, take it.

I don't know about you, but I don't want these things to stress me out or concern me. Sure, I want my home to function, to complete the tasks at hand, to live up to my responsibilities, and to live well for Him. But I don't want to freak out about the details. I want to hang out with Jesus and His loving-kindness—have it infuse my days, thank you very much.

I want to sing to Jesus while I prepare dinner (*in the evening when I cook*—it's fine, I make up lyrics to songs all the time), remembering Jesus provides the food, and He's cool with whatever vegetable I put out. He doesn't judge on those piddly things.

I want to chuckle with Jesus (*in the daytime as I sigh*) as I pass another burned-out light and hear Him whisper, "I am the light of the world" (John 8:12), and know in my heart that it's true. Sure, light bulbs are handy in Ohio, but the light I really need in my life is Jesus.

I want to put on my pj's, slide under my covers (*in the evening when I'm done*) and hear Him remind me,

"Come to me, all you who are weary and burdened, and I will give you rest" (Matthew 11:28).

I want to walk through my days, lists, triumphs, and losses with one anthem on my lips . . . *Give me Jesus!* When I rise. Or when I fall. When I'm alone. Or when I'm in a crowd.

Oh, when I come to die. Give me Jesus.

When I'm dying—dying laughing, dying because I tried to keep up with someone else, dying of shame, or actually struggling with an ailment that seems stronger than me—in all these times what I want most is Jesus. He is my strength and my hope.

Yes, there is pressure and worry in this life, but I do find heaps of happiness in the day-to-day. I don't think I could echo Solomon's words that "everything is meaningless," but maybe that's just because I'm on the lookout for Jesus. I think that's our goal as Christians. Because the more we seek Jesus, the more the thing we're wanting is Him. The more He can shine His love and grace on us. The more He can nurture and strengthen us. The more He can open our eyes, change our perspectives, and help us find true meaning in Him and all He offers.

When I'm eating kale or cookies, tromping up the stairs or going for a walk in the fresh air. No matter where we go or what we're doing, no matter if we feel like a wise king or a neglected servant—with Jesus, life is meaningful. Let's tell "them," shall we? You can have all this world. Give us Jesus.

CONTEMPLATE

We know that for those who love God all things work together for good, for those who are called according to his purpose. (Romans 8:28 ESV)

1. What do you think about when you first wake up?

2. What do you think about before you fall asleep?

3. Has there ever been a time when you wanted to throw up your hands (or your lunch) and say, "You can have this world!" When?

4. "Give Me Jesus" is a mantra we can have on repeat. How will you incorporate this phrase into your week? Try it below with something you might struggle with on a regular basis. Like: *When I drive carpool . . . give me Jesus!*

21

THE OLD RUGGED CROSS

George Bennard, written in 1913

On a hill far away stood an old rugged cross,
The emblem of suffering and shame;
And I love that old cross where the dearest and best
For a world of lost sinners was slain.

> *So I'll cherish the old rugged cross,*
> *Till my trophies at last I lay down;*
> *I will cling to the old rugged cross,*
> *And exchange it some day for a crown.*

Oh, that old rugged cross, so despised by the world,
Has a wondrous attraction for me;
For the dear Lamb of God left His glory above
To bear it to dark Calvary.

In that old rugged cross, stained with blood so
   divine,
A wondrous beauty I see,

For 'twas on that old cross Jesus suffered and died,
To pardon and sanctify me.

To the old rugged cross I will ever be true,
Its shame and reproach gladly bear;
Then He'll call me some day to my home far away,
Where His glory forever I'll share.

How Hymns Humble Us

There's a chest of drawers in our guest room cluttered with trophies—"Team with the Best Heart," "Runners-Up Western Buckeye League," "Champions Fill the Net Tournament." They are various shapes and sizes, mostly decorated with plastic golden soccer balls or smooth, shiny athletes in mid-kick. These trophies don't hold value for me because they were never prizes I sought.

However, when my kids won these trophies, the statues and medals symbolized major accomplishments for them. And even though three of my kids still play the game, these awards from previous seasons and teams seem trivial now. My kids have advanced to higher levels of competition. There are new goals to score, games to win, and tournaments to conquer.

A line from the hymn "The Old Rugged Cross" plays through my head as I consider toting the trophies to the trash: *Till my trophies at last I lay down.* But I don't do it. Even though these trophies have lost some shine to my kids, they're still not ready to "lay them down," let go of these symbols of accomplishment, these objects that testify to their self-worth.

And so it goes with our worldly trophies. We don't have to be kids in cleats to clutch our trophies. Our trophies could be a title at work, living in a certain neighborhood, being included in a specific group, achieving a coveted ranking, or selling, say, a certain number of books. (I'm just saying. Apparently this is important to some folks.) But these worldly trophies are no different than the plastic mementos from my kids' candy-league teams. We all have status symbols that make us feel we've arrived, we've achieved.

If we only did that, could afford that, earned that, made that, reached that . . . then we'd be successful, happy, satisfied—we'd matter. But honestly, we can chase after all those worldly idols (the irony of the trophies being golden statuettes does not elude me) 24-7 and never be fulfilled. Becoming vice president sparks our ambition to one day become president. Moving into the house of our dreams provides us incentive to decorate, remodel, and light cypress-scented candles as if we could earn a stamp of "beautiful enough" from Joanna Gaines. Working up our stamina to run three miles inspires us to sweat more, push our muscles harder, so we can run four miles and then five, six, a half marathon . . . get one of those 13.1 stickers for the back of our car.

Don't get me wrong. It's great to have goals. God calls us to do work for Him, provide for the people who depend on us, and take care of our bodies and homes. God has incredible plans for us. He nudges us out of our comfort zones. He asks us to bravely step forward in faith to push towards His goals. But achieving a mile-marker doesn't make us complete. There always seems to be another trophy to vie for.

Doesn't there?

Most detective shows end with the agent solving the crime, clinking glasses with their partner, sipping crisp bubbly champagne, and then with only two minutes remaining of the episode, receiving a message about their next mission. The agent cannot wait to run off and solve another mystery or take down another bad guy . . . to be continued. Musicians whose songs hit number one immediately jump back to the recording studio in hopes the next song will also top the charts. As soon as Elevation Worship released their album *There Is a Cloud*,[1] their pastor, Steven Furtick, asked, "What's next?" Teams who win the Super Bowl are pressured to become two-time national champions. Then to see how many rings they can collect.

We never seem to be satisfied.

Who says, "I don't need another trophy," let alone lays down the ones they've already won? The ultimate, as it turns out, is actually never enough. There's only one thing that is. Jesus.

As Paul says in his letter to the Galatians:

I tried keeping rules and working my head off to please God, and it didn't work. So I quit being a "law man" so that I could be *God's* man. Christ's life showed me how, and enabled me to do it. I identified

myself completely with Him. Indeed, I have been crucified with Christ. My ego is no longer central. It is
no longer important that I appear righteous before
you or have your good opinion, and I am no longer
driven to impress God. Christ lives in me. (Galatians
2:19–20 MSG)

Paul turned in his trophies—his expensive education
in the temple, impressive pedigree as a Jew, revered social
status as a Roman citizen—all of it, to follow Jesus. Those
things—his trophies, all the things Paul thought had mattered his entire life turned out to not be important at all.
Not to Paul. Not to God. The same holds true for us.

Are we working our heads off to please God and man?
What are we trying to prove? To who? Are we working
toward new trophies? Holding on to old ones?

When Christ lives in us, what we've achieved or what
our status is no longer matters. When God looks at us,
He sees perfect Jesus. There's nothing left to earn.

It boggles my brain.

We, who haven't quite arrived, or achieved that thing
everyone tells us is important, we count. We, who are still
climbing the ladder, doing the drills, studying, striving,
and to be honest just trying to keep it together most days,
we count. God sees us as perfect even though we're still
sanding out the rough spots, even though we're a tangled
mess. If you've asked Jesus into your life, He lives inside
you. And with the credentials of the King of Kings, the
Lord of Lords, the Alpha and the Omega, what could we
possibly be trying to prove that we don't already have?

Jesus gives us His crown.

We can wear it proudly and boldly.

Yes, we should still show up for work tomorrow, eat right, and be kind to our neighbors. Not to earn another gold star (we don't need those trophies anymore), but to show our love and appreciation for Jesus.

Don't worry. We don't have to move out of our cozy homes or quit our jobs, we just need to figuratively lay these things down, accept them as blessings from God, realize they don't define, inflate, or deflate our value. When we position these worldly achievements as gifts to be grateful for, we can trade how we used to see them (something we earned), for what they actually are—presents. And we can swap why we thought we needed our trophies, for what we really need and already have—Jesus.

This old hymn undoes me. I was trying to read the lyrics out loud to my family because I was so blown away by how this song, written more than one hundred years ago by George Bennard,[2] so clearly states the current dilemma of our culture, of my life, and I got through maybe ten words before my voice stopped working and my eyes blurred.

So I'll cherish the old rugged cross, till my trophies at last I lay down; I will cling to the old rugged cross, and exchange it some day for a crown.

When at last will I lay down all of my trophies—stop checking email to see if my proposal has been accepted, stop checking Instagram to see if I have any new followers, stop checking Amazon to see how my books rank?

I'm working on it.

On just hanging out with Jesus, remembering His perfect crown is on my head. On cherishing that love, and knowing it's more than enough. It's everything.

But, I am a work in progress.

Some days I lay those trophies down. They don't matter to me at all because they never should. But there are still plenty of insecure days, hesitant days, when I turn to my trophies to try to justify or remind myself that I have value. Those trophies will never do that. They can't.

Jesus can and will. Every. Single. Time.

So I cling to that old rugged cross, I'm desperately trying to hold on, no matter what good or bad happens in my world. Daily, I box up my trophies and take them out to the curb. Daily, I try to resist the temptation to go out and retrieve one from the box or take a picture of it to post or touch it just for a minute.

And daily, I praise Jesus that when I do lay down these trophies, in exchange He hands me an exquisite crown, one that reminds me He's already paid the price for my value, made me worthy, and whole. That He'll call me some day to my home far away, where His glory forever I'll share.

CONTEMPLATE

I have been crucified with Christ. My ego is no longer central. It is no longer important that I appear righteous before you or have your good opinion, and I am no longer driven to impress God. Christ lives in me. (Galatians 2:20 MSG)

1. What past accomplishments, "trophies," are you holding on to in your life? What would it take for you to lay them down? This could mean throwing away old awards from work or high school. It could mean changing your signature line on your emails. It could mean biting your tongue every time you're tempted to say, "My son is the quarterback" or "My husband set up this event" or "I actually won the award last year" or some such bragging rights.

2. Come up with an intentional plan to "lay down" at least one trophy this week. If it's easy, lay down another one or two.

22

SILENT NIGHT

Joseph Mohr in German, 1816 or 1818
First edition published in 1833
Translated into English in 1859 by John Freeman Young[1]

Silent night, holy night,
All is calm, all is bright
Round yon virgin mother and Child.
Holy Infant, so tender and mild,
Sleep in heavenly peace,
Sleep in heavenly peace.

Silent night, holy night,
Shepherds quake at the sight;
Glories stream from heaven afar,
Heavenly hosts sing Alleluia!
Christ the Savior is born,
Christ the Savior is born!

Silent night, holy night,
Son of God, love's pure light;
Radiant beams from thy holy face

With the dawn of redeeming grace,
Jesus, Lord, at thy birth,
Jesus, Lord, at thy birth.

How Hymns Bring Us Peace

Life is noisy.

The whirr of the dishwasher, the ding of the dryer, the buzz of texts, the various ring tones of calls, alarms, and timers, the beep of the microwave, the roar of fans and screams of coaches, hairdryers, food processors, electric toothbrushes, vacuums. And even when we find a moment where there doesn't have to be noise, we turn on the music or the TV or a podcast.

When was the last time you actually sat in silence?

Christmas is no different. Maybe even higher on the scale of noisiness—Salvation Army bells, jingle bells, sleigh bells, doorbells, bell-shaped sugar cookies spread with sweet, creamy frosting (okay, you got me, they don't make any noise, but how could we leave them out?), the bell choir at church, the mumbled voice of the drive-through worker at Taco Bell who sounds like Charlie Brown's teacher, but you shout your order to them anyway because with all the shopping, baking, and wrapping, who has time to make dinner?

One familiar Christmas song declares that over all the bustle you'll hear . . . bells.[2] And silver bells tinkling sound lovely, but even more powerful than another bell or chime in our lives is silence.

We just don't have very much of it. And when we do, it makes us a tad bit nervous. How long can you sit in silence . . . without grabbing your phone or a book or the remote? We're not good at it. But then again, civilized humanity has never been that good at silence. Even back in her time Jane Austen talks about the constant parlor chat used to "fill the air" in her novel *Mansfield Park*, when her character Edmund Bertram asks for something unusual: "Let us have the luxury of silence" (long before electronics and technology).[3]

Silence is a luxury. But we so rarely allow ourselves to sink into it unless we're asleep. Even in our unconscious state of rest we might turn on a fan or white noise machine for "background noise." More noise.

There was one night in history that was also extremely loud. The volume in the cities was turned up high due to the census. Citizens from all over flooded their towns of origin to be counted. Inns and guesthouses were full to overflowing. Streets were packed with out-of-towners, shuffling here and there, not knowing their way around. Food vendors shouted above one another, haggling with tourists, taking full advantage of the influx of customers. All of the excess people crowding the cities brought with them horses and donkeys, neighing and braying.

But on this same night everything changed forever. This night was holier than any other. More powerful than any other. It was the night the promises of the prophets were fulfilled. The night God sliced through the divide of God and man. God sent His only Son, Jesus, down to earth, to live and love His people face-to-face.

Emmanuel. God with us. In the flesh.

And in that instant all the noise, the stress of traveling, the complaining of sore feet, the bickering between exhausted family members, the growling of hungry stomachs, the stamping of unsettled animals went mute. The dark moods of sojourners lifted. The dark back alleys of town illuminated.

All was calm. All was bright.

Do you crave that?

In the midst of the craziness, the busyness, the to-do lists, and the noise? A breath of peace, of silence, of brightness?

The first few notes of "Silent Night" allow for this. Although there are differing stories as to the hymn's origin, it appears an Austrian parish priest named Joseph Mohr originally wrote this hymn as a poem in 1816. A couple years later it was first played with music. It seems a church's organ broke, and thus the church needed a beautiful and peaceful song that could be played on guitar for Christmas Eve. The priest gave his poem to a friend named Franz Gruber, who was his organist. Though it was a bit of a scramble, they got their arrangement completed in time for midnight mass, and this hymn has been ushering in the peace of Christmas for more than two hundred years ever since.[4]

The opening lyrics *Silent night, holy night* remove us from the hustle and bustle and allow us to inhale.

And exhale.

The next line *All is calm, all is bright* disintegrates the urgency of shopping and the stress over who was and wasn't included on our Christmas card lists. And as all the noise of the holiday season dissolves, we're led to the actual manger.

Holy Infant, so tender and mild.

Can you smell the sweet fragrance of hay?

Can you see Him? Sweet baby Jesus, snuggled up, eyes gently closed, chest rising up and down in stress-free slumber. The epitome of peace. The thing you've been truly longing for all your life.

And just as we're finally finding a moment of rest in this tranquil scene, the next verse reminds us why we feel so serene in this ancient stable.

Glories stream from heaven afar.

Can you see the golden rays of light illuminating the baby's face, revealing that this isn't just the sweet innocence of a newborn that brings us peace, but something so much more powerful? Something that comes only from God. Only from God's love for us. And in the midst of the quiet, we hear something, but oddly the *heavenly hosts* singing *Alleluia* doesn't disrupt the peace. Although the company of heavenly hosts must have shaken the stable, their triumphant song actually adds to our inner stillness because it highlights the holiness of the moment. And the glow in the room, now in our hearts, this inner joy, this sense that all is right in the world, can only come from one place.

Love's pure light.

The shepherds at the scene quaked. Mary looked on pondering all of these things in her heart. But we get a bigger view.

We feel the overwhelming tide of joy and gratitude that God fulfilled His promises; He sent the Messiah to the world, to Bethlehem, from the line of David, just as He had promised for centuries. We feel the rush of relief and the desire to bow down to worship the God who never forgot His people, who always keeps His promises. But even though we sometimes wish we could have been there that night, long to have been an eyewitness to the Savior's birth, we have been gifted with so much more. We get an even more glorious Christmas gift. We get the benefit of seeing and hearing how it all played out in the Scriptures.

We know Mary was there when Jesus was crucified, but we don't have any idea if those shepherds were there some thirty-three years later. Other folks crowded in to Bethlehem that night for the census, those who might have heard the angels singing or overheard people talking in the streets about the Messiah being born, about the spectacle happening just outside of town in a stable. These folks may or may not have recognized Jesus as a man. They might or might not have connected the dots to that incredible occurrence the year of the census with all the buzz about the rabbi who was crucified, a tomb found empty, the stories of Him being resurrected and appearing to hundreds of people.

But we get to see it all.

We get to see Christmas and Easter. The birth in the stable, and what Jesus went through for us on the cross. We get to see that not only did He come down to live among us, and to teach us, but also to offer us living water, new life, and ultimately redemption.

The night Jesus was born was *the dawn of redeeming grace*. And we are privy to the whole story—to how it ends. But in the midst of our noise we sometimes lose sight of it. The hymn "Silent Night" allows us to go back to page one of our redemption stories, to remember again the moment Jesus chose to do this thing that would silence our fear, pain, anxiety, stress, shame, and loneliness forever.

This silence is worth seeking. Worth turning everything else down to hear, to absorb, to sit in awe and wonder. To remember that even though life on earth is sometimes harmful, hurtful, and incredibly noisy, when we focus on Jesus, once again all can be calm, all can be bright.

CONTEMPLATE

So they hurried off and found Mary and Joseph, and the baby, who was lying in the manger. When they had seen him, they spread the word concerning what had been told them about this child, and all who heard it were amazed at what the shepherds said to them. But Mary treasured up all these things and pondered them in her heart. The shepherds returned, glorifying and praising God for all the things they had heard and seen, which were just as they had been told. (Luke 2:16–20)

1. How often do you find silence in your life?

2. How can you find time this week to be still and silent with the Lord?

23

HE WILL HOLD ME FAST

Ada R. Habershon, 1906

When I fear my faith will fail,
Christ will hold me fast;
When the tempter would prevail,
He can hold me fast.

> *He will hold me fast,*
> *He will hold me fast;*
> *For my Savior loves me so,*
> *He will hold me fast.*

I could never keep my hold,
He will hold me fast;
For my love is often cold,
He must hold me fast.

I am precious in His sight,
He will hold me fast;
Those He saves are His delight,
He will hold me fast.

He'll not let my soul be lost,
Christ will hold me fast;
Bought by Him at such a cost,
He will hold me fast.

How Hymns Soothe Us

I walk into church my mind spinning. My oldest is home from college for the weekend, and I was so looking forward to her visit. But she's overwhelmed by the assignments she brought home to work on and the event she's planning for her sorority. I want this service to be good for her exhausted soul. I want the sermon to ring true and the worship band to play all her favorite songs. I pray for all of this as she sets down her mocha under the seat in front of her and tucks her blonde hair behind her right ear.

God, please help her find you here today.

The book I've been working on got cancelled yesterday. The publisher had a staffing upheaval, and with it a reduction of new titles. Including mine.

God, I thought you wanted me to write this book. I thought you gave me the green light. What now?

My teenage son strums the opening song on his acoustic guitar from the stage, and I pray that he can play his best, be confident in who God made him to be, and in his ability to play with the band despite how much younger he is than anyone else up there.

God, please let him know you're with him up there.

There's drama surrounding my high school girl. She's funny, kind, and works her tail off to excel at school, in her sports, and in her relationships. She puts so much pressure on herself. I pray for her, that she can know best how to handle the boys and the friends and the sports and the classes and balance all the things she wants to do with all the things she needs to get done, but mainly that she can lean into Jesus, trust in Him.

Jesus, please help her stick to you like glue.

And my youngest—still a little boy in many ways, but also on the verge of growing up. He'll leave the sanctuary during the sermon to meet with the other middle schoolers and hear a lesson from the youth pastor. I pray it will feed him in the way his intelligent, loving self needs to be fed. But also my mama heart is a bit tangled because it's the end of November, and I'm pretty sure he still believes in Santa, and he's way past the age but has such a tender, creative soul that he, like me, sees magic anywhere he can. I should probably tell him, but I don't want to be the one to break his heart.

Jesus, please hold his little not-so-little self.

My husband, handsome and steady, puts his hand on the small of my back. I hear his voice singing along, and I'm grateful we're here together, that we both love Jesus. I have so many friends whose marriages are in turmoil or they've never found a soul mate or they've lost the one they loved. I pray for them, and for my marriage, that I can be a good wife to this amazing man because, *ugh*, I fall short everyday—rolling my eyes, shaking my head, preferring my ways to his.

God, please help me love him better.

I feel unsettled, all shaken up in my soul, and not in a good way. Nothing seems to be in place, and I don't feel like I can control any of it.

That's it right there—out of control.

I hate being out of control, and I currently am. So, I pray all these things, but they're more like lists I'm going through—"God, help this person, fix that, improve me . . ."—demands even, like when I ask my kids to take out the trash or put their backpacks away: "Do this, then that, and when you're finished with that . . ."

And just like I feel the need to follow up on my kids—make sure their lunch was actually packed—I feel like I need to trail behind God, reminding Him of what needs to be done. *Yuck!*

So now, I've sung the first worship song, tried to focus on the words, tried to let the music center me, but I still feel cluttered inside. I haven't let go of anything. I'm holding on to everything, but don't have any idea how to fix any of it. I'm talking at God, but not hearing Him, probably because I'm not even trying to listen.

Ever had one of those days?

Then the lyrics to "He Will Hold Me Fast" by Ada Habershon appear on the screen. An old hymn written in 1906 we haven't sung here before, but still the words seem familiar.[1] They must hold some little piece of real estate in my memory. I sing the first few lines like a robot and then get to the refrain, *He will hold me fast, He will hold me fast; for my Savior loves me so, He will hold me fast.*

I sense God answering my list o' prayers, not with specific responses to my multiple demands; He's wiser than that. He simply addresses all my concerns with one whispered phrase, *I will hold you fast.*

And I lose it.

He will hold me.

He is holding me.

Why do I feel responsible for everything? Why am I allowing the enemy to fill my head with so many worries that were never my responsibility to begin with? Why am I not trusting God to be in control? Where is my faith?

When I fear my faith will fail, Christ will hold me fast; when the tempter would prevail, He can hold me fast.

As I continue singing, my prayers change. I go from handing God a list of chores that I'm not even trusting Him to execute, to thanking Him for who He is and how He loves. A God who holds me in the everyday, in all the days. A God who will take the wheel because He is a way better driver.

Peace washes over me.

In my heart I pray, "Jesus, you are in charge. You are my peace. I have no need to worry because you love my kids, my husband, me. You are holding them all fast, tightly in your arms. I pray they will tangibly feel that, feel you. I pray I can drink in this truth—this security, and stop fussing. That's my actual prayer, God. If you can soothe me so sweetly with a song, then you can do the same for them. And with you holding on to all of us? All the other things fall into place. No matter how hectic, challenging, or confusing life seems, I feel calm because you are in control. You hold me fast. Whew."

My concerns on this random Sunday are trivial, yet these are the things that keep me up at night. I love the work God has commissioned me to do, and want to do it well for Him. As an Enneagram Two with a One-Wing[2] I would do anything for my family and to a fault feel like their happiness and wholeness depends on how well I perform in the caring-for-them department. I know with my head that it doesn't all fall on me, but my heart tends to forget.

This hymn, "He Will Hold Me Fast," shifts the responsibility for my family's joy from me to Jesus. And honestly, He is far better suited for the job.

He'll not let my soul be lost; Christ will hold me fast; bought by Him at such a cost, He will hold me fast.

Jesus wants us and our families to see Him, feel Him, trust Him. This is my greatest prayer, but it's God's strong desire too. He won't let go. The Lord will keep His promises not just to me, but to my husband, each of my kids, to you, and your people. Shifting our gaze toward Jesus shifts everything else too. It changes our fears into trust, morphs our concerns into sighs of relief, deflates our stress until it feels more like peace, soothes us. As King David writes in Psalm 30:11, "You turned my wailing into dancing; you removed my sackcloth and clothed me with joy."

Jesus loves the people we love, so much that He laid down His life for them. Jesus created our friends and family and all of creation. He created our passions and vocations and will assign us the work accordingly.

"Pray as if everything depended on God and work as if everything depended on you" is a quote usually attributed to Ignatius of Loyola. This is something I try to apply to my life. The problem is, I work like crazy, pray fervently, and then still feel like I'm responsible to get it all done. I'd like to add another line: "then trust God to do it."

Because God is there for us. Always. No matter where we go—high or low, deep or wide. He is there, holding us.

King David also wrote:

> If I rise on the wings of the dawn,
>   if I settle on the far side of the sea,
> even there your hand will guide me,
>   your right hand will hold me fast. (Psalm 139:9–10)

I like the Message version of these verses:

> If I flew on morning's wings
>   to the far western horizon,
> You'd find me in a minute—
>   you're already there waiting! (Psalm 139:9–10 MSG)

God will find us in a minute. No matter where we are. In fact, He's already waiting for us.

And this isn't just Old Testament. We see this same truth in Paul's letter to the Romans:

> For I am convinced that neither death nor life, nei-
> ther angels nor demons, neither the present nor the
> future, nor any powers, neither height nor depth, nor

anything else in all creation, will be able to separate us from the love of God that is in Christ Jesus our Lord. (Romans 8:38–39)

We don't need to fret—even when we don't know how to help or what's next. God is sticking with us. Holding us fast. Nothing can separate us from Him.

Is it good to recognize our needs and the needs of those around us? Absolutely. Does God want us to ask Him for help? Of course. But then He wants us to trust Him to take it from there. We can trust Him. Christ will guide us, give us the words, the ideas, build into our relationships, rescue us and the ones we love. He will hold us fast.

I am precious in His sight, He will hold me fast; Those He saves are His delight, He will hold me fast.

CONTEMPLATE

If I rise on the wings of the dawn,
    if I settle on the far side of the sea,
even there your hand will guide me,
    your right hand will hold me fast. (Psalm 139:9–10)

1. What concerns or prayers are swirling through your brain in this season? Jot at least three of them down.

2. God sees us everywhere we go. He sees our loved ones, and where their feet lead them. Next to the concerns you wrote down above write: *God sees me. He will hold me fast.* For example, I could write: *I'm*

worried about my oldest. She's so stressed out and tense. I want her to find peace, relax, let go, and get a good night's sleep. And then write, *God sees her and all of the things stressing her out. He will hold her fast.*

24

BLESSED ASSURANCE

Fanny Crosby, 1873

Blessed assurance, Jesus is mine!
O what a foretaste of glory divine!
Heir of salvation, purchase of God,
Born of His Spirit, washed in His blood.

> *This is my story, this is my song,*
> *Praising my Savior, all the day long;*
> *This is my story, this is my song,*
> *Praising my Savior, all the day long.*

Perfect submission, perfect delight!
Visions of rapture now burst on my sight;
Angels descending bring from above
Echoes of mercy, whispers of love.

Perfect submission, all is at rest!
I in my Savior am happy and blessed,
Watching and waiting, looking above,
Filled with His goodness, lost in His love.

How Hymns Tell Our Story

When I was little I devoured the true tales of Laura Ingalls Wilder living in her *Little House on the Prairie*. I even convinced my mom to make "snow candy" like my namesake, Laura, pouring hot, thick, sweet syrup onto the frozen snow. I also read and reread the story of Charlotte the spider weaving "Some Pig" into her delicate web among the rafters to save her friend Wilber.

I checked out as many books as my mom would allow me at the library. When I read through those, I took to reading every book I could find in our house, fingering the Braille-like raised lettering on their spines, a secret language speaking to my heart. I've always loved books and been fascinated by the worlds inside them.

Each of us has an incredible story. Sometimes they're tricky to spot from the outside, but if you dig a bit, you can turn up something remarkable about everyone you meet, something that would fill the pages of a book and delight a reader.

One of my kid's teachers has thirteen siblings. Can you imagine? Being the mom of fourteen kids—getting them out the door for school in the mornings? Making sure everyone brushed their teeth and had on matching socks? Can you imagine a book about the conversations between all of those kids growing up?

A friend of mine used to tour the world singing opera. Plus, her husband gets to vote for the Grammy Awards every year! I want to vote for the Grammy Awards. Okay, actually I don't care if I get to vote, but they also get to attend the Grammys every year, and I really want to do that. An inside peek into the music industry—the stars, the fashion—from my friend's viewpoint could be a best seller. As could the tales of her traveling from country to country singing in Italian. She tells of the romances between lead singers, the rivalry amongst star vocalists. Page-turner.

Everybody has a story.

What's yours?

The hymn "Blessed Assurance" speaks to our story as Christians: *This is my story, this is my song, praising my Savior, all the day long.* This is a story believers in Jesus get to share.

We all have families of origin, the neighborhoods we grew up in, traditions, experiences, skills, and people we've met that help form our stories. I'm the youngest, have a killer chocolate chip cookie recipe, have memorized the text of Dr. Seuss's *How the Grinch Stole Christmas*, am allergic to fire ants, prefer beaches to ski slopes, and have divorced parents.

You have different chapters.

But the critical part of our story is shared, woven into our very fabric. It is not a random detail like we both love koala bears (how cute and cuddly are they?). It's the most critical part of our stories, the piece that defines us—the cross. The true story that God loved us so much He decided to send His only Son, Jesus, down to earth to live among us, and then die to erase all of our sins, so we could live with Him happily ever after (John 3:16, translation mine).

The lyrics to "Blessed Assurance," that we're *born of His Spirit, washed in His blood,* speak to pages in our life books about our salvation: *This is my story, this is my song.* And because this is our story, the thing we should be most drawn to is *praising* our *Savior, all the day long.*

Yes, many more paragraphs, scenes and chapters will be written over the years to our personal narratives. We'll get transferred, discover the wonders of an entirely new place, develop a physical challenge, change churches, make a new friend, have a falling out, hear a speaker who inspires us, get a puppy, lose a loved one, pick up a tennis racquet—all these things will stretch, grow, and mold our characters, adding new pages to our stories.

And when we discover that new favorite spot, trail, recipe, activity, or face, we can be blessedly assured Jesus did that for us so we could find joy. In those chapters of life where we move to a new city or a friend moves away, we can be blessedly assured that Jesus is with us. In the pages where we struggle to communicate or are connecting with someone new, when we're navigating our relationships, we can be blessedly assured we don't need to impress Jesus—He loves us for exactly who we are. With every new chapter if we look to Jesus, hold Him close, we can sing in good times and bad: *I in my Savior am happy and blessed.*

We're reminded in Scripture that we are "a chosen people, a royal priesthood, a holy nation, God's special possession, that you may declare the praises of him who called you out of darkness into his wonderful light" (1 Peter 2:9).

So, yes, even in the dark scenes of our tales, Jesus's wonderful light is there for us.

I have this crazy hour in the evenings when all the kids get home from school, but three have to be somewhere—practice, youth group, babysitting—and they're all leaving at different times, and I need to get dinner on the table so they can eat before they go. But one of them needs help with the printer, and another can't find batteries for his calculator, and a third is arguing with a friend. Then my mom calls. And my husband asks if "we" (meaning "me") have paid a specific bill. And I feel like I'll scream, implode, or throw something. All of which would be really bad.

So, I exit the kitchen where all the madness is going down, and step onto our screened in porch. Even in February. Even in a rainstorm. And I ask Jesus for peace. "Please calm me," I beg. Sometimes I can't even form words, except for His name. Jesus.

And there on my porch, God meets me. He uses the crisp air against my skin, or the inviting hazy scent of our neighbor's fireplace, or the patter of rain to turn the page—to get my attention off my stress and back to Him, the Creator of fire and wind. And when I lean into Him, the panic ebbs, and I can be *filled with His goodness, lost in His love.* It washes over me. Changes me. Refreshes and renews me. He offers this to all of us when we intentionally seek Him.

And that space of being filled with Christ's goodness, lost in His love? *Sigh.* That's a page of my story I want to linger over. I want to reread that page again and again.

And it reminds me that this isn't just a page of my story, it is my plotline. A story of love and sacrifice and devotion, of a Lord and Creator who would do all that for me, for you. That every page of my story, from when I climbed the giant willow tree in the field behind our house as a girl, to when I sell concessions at my son's basketball game this afternoon, is written by God, the Author of the universe.

For each and every experience we have, every chapter of our stories, the blessed assurance that Jesus was and is and will be walking with us is ours.

And because His love is written onto every page of our lives, when we receive the bad news, get invited to lead the group, the water heater dies, celebrate our anniversaries, no matter if we're in a troubling or triumphant chapter, we can sing, *This is my story, this is my song.* And because we have the blessed assurance that our story says we're saved, redeemed, and rescued by Jesus, we don't have to worry about tomorrow's plot twists. We can relax with Jesus today and be *praising* our *Savior, all the day long.*

CONTEMPLATE

You are a chosen people, a royal priesthood, a holy nation, God's special possession, that you may declare the praises of him who called you out of darkness into his wonderful light. (1 Peter 2:9)

1. What are some specific pages of your life story that make it unique?

2. What are some challenges you've faced in your personal narrative?

3. As you travel through this chapter of your life, where do you want to remind yourself of the "blessed assurance" that Jesus loves you and walks with you this week?

25

GO, TELL IT ON
THE MOUNTAIN

African American spiritual,
dating back at least to 1865
Compiled by John Wesley Work Jr.,
first published in 1907

Go, tell it on the mountain,
Over the hills and everywhere.
Go, tell it on the mountain,
That Jesus Christ is born.

While shepherds kept their watching
O'er silent flocks by night,
Behold throughout the heavens
There shone a holy light.

The shepherds feared and trembled,
When lo! above the earth,
Rang out the angel chorus
That hailed the Savior's birth.

Down in a lowly manger
The humble Christ was born,
And God sent us salvation
That blessed Christmas morn.

How Hymns Help Us Share the Gospel

"I need you," my son's vocal coach's harmony mingles with my son's melody. I'm in the other room with a novel I brought to read during his lesson. The pages sit open on my lap, but I'm not reading. I can't. The song they're singing, "Whole Heart" by Hillsong United,[1] is too beautiful, too magnetic, and pulls me out of my book and into the lyrics. Last week his teacher, Lisa,* said to us as we were leaving, "That is such a powerful song. I can't get it out of my head."

Did I mention Lisa's not a Christian?

And yet, this song about Jesus restoring our brokenness through His grace is stuck in Lisa's head. She's singing it out loud, over and over. Words about clinging to the rock, about being made whole—an anthem so fitting for Lisa.

Her husband passed away three years ago. I'm not sure how old she is. Late fifties? Too young to be widowed. Any age is too young to be widowed. And she lives in the beautiful home they built together, teaching music because it's her passion. Lisa is kind and encouraging and every flavor of loveliness, but she doesn't know Jesus.

*This name has been changed to protect the individual's privacy.

She's shared with me how much she misses her husband, how difficult it is. And then my son (I'm actually going to assume it was the Spirit prompting my son) picks this song as the piece he wants to work on. A song about Jesus pulling us upright when we're too weak to stand.

Beautiful, isn't it?

That's why I can't read today—can't pull myself away from the marvel of a woman learning about Jesus, experiencing who He is, feeling the tug of His love. My eyes are closed. Still a tear leaks out of the right corner and glides down my cheek.

This is what sharing the gospel looks like—beautiful, moving, real. There's an old spiritual that was passed among the plantations in the South called "Go, Tell It on the Mountain."

Go, tell it on the mountain, over the hills and everywhere. Go, tell it on the mountain, that Jesus Christ is born.

Jesus calls us to this. His final conversation with the disciples (recorded in Matthew 28:19, Luke 24:47, and Acts 1:8) is Jesus instructing them (and now us) to tell the whole world about Him.

And you will be my witnesses, telling people about me everywhere—in Jerusalem, throughout Judea, in Samaria, and to the ends of the earth. (Acts 1:8 NLT)

Telling the whole earth about Jesus, *over the hills and everywhere*, sounds difficult, especially in our do-it-yourself culture. Where do we start? With whom? When? Under what circumstances?

In the early 1900s, even acquiring and writing down the lyrics to "Go, Tell It on the Mountain" was a challenge. The song had been passed along verbally. There was no written record of it. As you can imagine there were several versions being sung. But John Wesley Work Jr. was passionate about collecting and preserving African American spirituals so they could be shared with people everywhere. His desire to distribute these songs proclaiming that *God sent us salvation that blessed Christmas morn* allows us to sing these hymns and contemplate their messages today.

Collecting scores of unwritten songs composed by slaves, verifying words, stanzas, and melodies from the Civil War era seemed unlikely, intimidating, and maybe not super popular with early-twentieth-century American culture. But to John Wesley Work Jr. it made sense. He was a highly educated man,[2] led the church choir, adored Jesus, and loved music. Curating and publishing books featuring the hymns of his ancestors was meaningful. Work included "Go, Tell It on the Mountain" in his second book, *Folk Songs of the American Negro.*[3]

This was such a natural way for Work to share the gospel.

Similarly, a high school boy sharing how Jesus can change your life with his vocal coach in a college town today also sounds unlikely, intimidating, and a little strange. But, sharing the gospel doesn't have to feel weird. My son didn't pull out a tract, recite verses, or tell Lisa a story about the time he accepted Jesus at camp.

Don't get me wrong. I write Christian content for a living, love memorizing Scripture, and actually accepted Christ at horseback riding camp in junior high.

I'm just saying we overthink this "Go tell the world" thing. We sometimes try too hard. Overanalyze.

Max is taking voice lessons so he can improve his worship leading skills in the band at our church. His teacher asked him what song he'd like to work on. Max suggested this one by Hillsong. He was just honest about the kind of music he listens to, the kind he sings—worship music. It was normal, natural, unforced. The next thing you know, this lovely lady is singing to Jesus.

I don't know if Lisa will accept Christ into her heart. But that's not my job or Max's. Telling people about Jesus, sharing who He is, that's our assignment—the Great Commission. John Wesley Work Jr. probably died having no idea how many people came to Christ because of the books of spirituals he published. But his job was to get them in print, get them out there, plant the seeds through songs.

As Max and I walk to the car we hear Lisa's alto trill across the walk declaring how God's grace holds her. Yes it does, my friend. Grace holds you, Lisa. Grace holds all of us. Me. Max. You, on the other side of this book. Grace holds you.

What a gorgeous truth.

I am so grateful God allowed Max to share Christ's grace with Lisa, maybe not on a mountain or in Judea, but on a piano bench in Oxford, Ohio. Because this is what Jesus asks us to do . . . go out and make disciples of all the nations. There's not a perfect way to do it. You don't have to have things written out or know all the answers. You just have to walk around loving Jesus. The rest will come naturally. You'll find your own mountains. And there you can tell others of His love.

CONTEMPLATE

And you will be my witnesses, telling people about me everywhere—in Jerusalem, throughout Judea, in Samaria, and to the ends of the earth. (Acts 1:8 NLT)

1. What are things you naturally do that share Jesus— play Christian radio in your car? Pray before meals? Wear a cross necklace? List some.

2. As you go about your week, how can you plant seeds of faith doing your normal, natural things? This could be meeting a friend for lunch and stating that you are going to pray before you eat. You don't have to force them to join in, but intentionally close your eyes, bow your head, and speak a few words of thanks. Write down something and commit to it.

26

'TIS SO SWEET
TO TRUST IN JESUS

Louisa M. R. Stead, 1882

'Tis so sweet to trust in Jesus,
Just to take Him at His Word;
Just to rest upon His promise,
Just to know, "Thus says the Lord!"

> *Jesus, Jesus, how I trust Him!*
> *How I've proved Him o'er and o'er*
> *Jesus, Jesus, precious Jesus!*
> *O for grace to trust Him more!*

O how sweet to trust in Jesus,
Just to trust His cleansing blood;
Just in simple faith to plunge me
'Neath the healing, cleansing flood!

Yes, 'tis sweet to trust in Jesus,
Just from sin and self to cease;

Just from Jesus simply taking
Life and rest, and joy and peace.

I'm so glad I learned to trust thee,
Precious Jesus, Savior, Friend;
And I know that thou art with me,
Wilt be with me to the end.

How Hymns Sustain Us

Our pastor tugged his auburn beard and took a long audible inhale as the band exited the stage.

"Our church is a family," he said. "And sometimes families need to address family business." He paused and shoved his hands into the front pockets of his jeans, as if deciding how to word what he would say next.

"I'm saddened to tell you one of our staff members was arrested over the weekend. He has been removed from his ministry duties for a few months. During that time the elders will be meeting with him in prayer and counseling." In the heavy silence that filled the sanctuary like smog, he shifted his weight. "It's all so recent; we're not really sure what happens next. But we do know we expect everyone to extend grace to this man and his family. Because Jesus offers us all grace."

Somehow our pastor managed to segue into prayer and then his sermon on the Holy Spirit, but my thoughts lingered on the man who had been arrested. I wanted to offer him forgiveness, because I have messed up plenty.

Let's just say I wouldn't want my sins announced in the front of church. I reminded myself in my head *I am a sinner saved by grace* as a defense against any judgment my thoughts might try to form against the reprimanded staff member.

But forgiveness and trust are not always one and the same. I found I *could* forgive him. He's human. He made a mistake, and got caught. But could I trust him again? I wanted to, but I wasn't sure.

What happened? We'd laughed with him and his wife. Prayed with them. Held their baby. He'd given my kids rides. He knew our stories. We were hurt and confused in ways we weren't sure how to address.

But I'm not the only one who has been let down. Everywhere we turn, allegations are being spewed against politicians, coaches, teachers, and leaders. Their poor decisions affect so many who know them, who were relying on them, depending on them. I've certainly made my own bad choices over the years and let down my share of folks who were counting on me. It saddens my heart to think about anyone I may have hurt. I pray God's grace will fill the gaps I've created.

If most of us have been let down and let others down— who can we trust?

Louisa Stead answers this question with the hymn she wrote, "'Tis So Sweet to Trust in Jesus."[1] When my heart aches with disappointment, her hymn is like a soothing balm, *Jesus, Jesus, how I trust him! How I've proved him o'er and o'er! Jesus, Jesus, precious Jesus! O for grace to trust him more!*

Has anyone you've trusted ever broadcast something you shared with them in confidence? Done something unthinkable? Lied to you? Said they would be there, but weren't? Jesus gets it. He's been through it himself. Some of the people nearest and dearest to Christ betrayed Him.

On the evening of the last supper Jesus sat around eating dinner with his closest friends. He humbly washed their feet. Can you imagine how dusty, sweaty, and smelly those men's feet must have been from walking the dirty streets of Jerusalem in sandals? Jesus then asked His friends to treat others with similar humility and kindness. In this sweet emotional bonding time we might expect a group hug or perhaps a toast? *Cheers!* But no. That's not how it went down. Jesus put away the soap, water, and towel and sat. Then the tone in the room changed.

> Now Jesus was deeply troubled, and he exclaimed, "I tell you the truth, one of you will betray me!" (John 13:21 NLT)

What? They were gathered for a meal. The disciples had been at Jesus's side for three years! Watching Him heal the blind, the lame, the lepers, the sick. They'd heard His teachings. They'd even declared they believed He was the long-awaited Messiah who would save their people. And yet one of them would betray Him? How could that be?

But we know it's true. Judas Iscariot, one of Jesus's twelve best friends, betrayed Jesus that very night.

Judas wasn't the only one. Just a few moments later Jesus told another member of His inner circle that he would turn against Him.

I tell you the truth, Peter—before the rooster crows tomorrow morning, you will deny three times that you even know me. (John 13:38 NLT)

Yikes!

Two of Jesus's best friends. On the hardest night of His life. They shunned Him. Peter pretended not once, but three times, that he didn't even know Jesus. And Judas, sold out Jesus for a handful of silver.

Jesus loved these men. He spent years walking, eating, praying, and talking with them. He'd saved them from storms, fed them when they were hungry, counseled them, pulled them out of where they'd been and shown them glorious love. And yet, Judas and Peter were human, flawed, like the rest of us. And they let the man they loved most down.

How did Jesus react?

The next words out of Jesus's mouth, after telling Peter how he would deny Him, were these: "Don't let your hearts be troubled. Trust in God, and trust also in me" (John 14:1 NLT).

Trust in Him. That's what Jesus suggests we do when we're troubled. When we feel let down. When we feel so betrayed that we don't even know how to respond.

Has someone you trusted disappointed you? Someone in authority? A leader? A close friend? Someone you confided in? Someone you love? Jesus sees you in this heartache. He truly understands. And when we feel like we're in a free fall, He reaches out and catches us, reminding us there is One we can always trust.

'Tis so sweet to trust in Jesus, just to take him at his word; just to rest upon his promise, and to know, "Thus saith the Lord!"

Disappointments in this life abound. But Jesus never fails us. He will always be strong enough, wise enough, loving enough to cover all of our needs. He will never leave our sides. Never ask us to do more than we can handle. Never condemn us.

As the author of the book of Hebrews states,

God has said, "Never will I leave you; never will I forsake you." (13:5)

Jesus Christ is the same yesterday and today and forever. (13:8)

There's such sweet relief in these statements. We don't have to worry if one day Jesus is going to do something that lets us down.

He won't.

When others abandon us Jesus never will. The things we know about Jesus, the things the Bible says about Him aren't going to change. Ever.

I'm so glad I learned to trust thee, precious Jesus, Savior, Friend. And I know that thou art with me, wilt be with me to the end.

I'm praying for healing and restoration, and I feel the Spirit at work. But I'm not sure how the current circumstances will affect this staff member, our church, or our family's relationship with him in the long run. Only time will tell. But I do know one thing. No matter where the future leads us, I can always trust in Jesus. And so can you. He promises to never change.

CONTEMPLATE

Don't let your hearts be troubled. Trust in God, and trust also in me. (John 14:1 NLT)

1. Has anyone you relied on ever let you down? If so, how did you feel?

2. Do you trust Jesus? That He will never leave you? Always love you? If you do, write below "I trust you, Jesus." And any time this week when things feel uncertain or overwhelming, why not say out loud, or write down again, "I trust you, Jesus."

3. If you're struggling to trust Jesus, why not ask Him right now to grow your trust. You could write this phrase out instead of the one above. "Jesus, please help me grow my trust in you and your constant love. Amen." Just like above, any time this week you feel wobbly, try saying or writing out this prayer to increase your trust again.

27

THIS LITTLE LIGHT OF MINE

Harry Dixon Loes, 1920s[1]

This little light of mine
I'm gonna let it shine
This little light of mine
I'm gonna let it shine
This little light of mine
I'm gonna let it shine
Let it shine let it shine let it shine

Hide it under a bushel no
I'm gonna let it shine
Hide it under a bushel no
I'm gonna let it shine
Hide it under a bushel no
I'm gonna let it shine
Let it shine let it shine let it shine

Don't let Satan blow it out
I'm gonna let it shine
Don't let Satan blow it out
I'm gonna let it shine
Don't let Satan blow it out
I'm gonna let it shine
Let it shine let it shine let it shine

Let it shine till Jesus comes
I'm gonna let it shine
Let it shine tell Jesus comes
I'm gonna let it shine
Let it shine tell Jesus comes
I'm gonna let it shine
Let it shine let it shine let it shine

How Hymns Ignite Us

Bright spotlights highlight an actor on stage. Christmas lights twinkle creating ambiance during the holidays. Special red light bulbs give photographers visibility while developing film the old-fashioned way in a darkroom. Traffic lights tell us when it's safe to stop or go. Night-lights keep the monsters at bay in a little one's bedroom. Flashlights send their narrow beam helping us forge a safe path when the power goes out. Candles flicker creating a soft glow and the comforting sweet scent of vanilla in a room. Stars illuminate the sky. All these lights possess a wide range of differing features, but they're still all lights. All of them were created differently to serve diverse purposes.

Just like us.

This little light of mine. I'm gonna let it shine.

Did you ever sing this song when you were little? Maybe at a "concert" for your parents? You held up your index finger in front of you pretending it was a candle and belted out the words. This hymn is all about us being lights. And it's as powerful and pertinent in our adult lives as it was to our kindergarten days. Maybe even more so.

Jesus tells us we are lights. "You're here to be light, bringing out the God-colors in the world" (Matthew 5:14 MSG).

The cool thing is, we all get to be different kinds of lights—some soft and glowing, others bright and powerful, some directive, others soothing, some to help things be found, illuminate the way, get the work done, or direct attention. None of our job descriptions as lights are any better or worse than anyone else's. They are all necessary for their specific purpose.

The apostle Paul explains it in his letter to the Romans like this:

> For just as each of us has one body with many members, and these members do not all have the same function, so in Christ we, though many, form one body, and each member belongs to all the others. We have different gifts, according to the grace given to each of us. (Romans 12:4–6)

You've seen others letting their lights shine, right?

The basketball player dribbling up and down the vacant court, back and forth, forward, and back again. Right hand. Left hand. When nobody is watching. When no one else is there. Not because dribbling is glamorous. But because it is necessary. And when that player goes into the game, he's not a ball hog. He's not lazy. He gets the ball where it needs to go—whether that's to a teammate, away from the opponent, or right in the basket. *Swoosh!* Because he's been working hard. Practicing. Over and over. Giving it his all. When he's interviewed for the school yearbook or blog or *Sports Illustrated*, he gives God the glory. He uses his inner light, and showcases it to show others how to work hard, be a team player, and use the gifts they've been given to glorify God. He lets his light shine. On a basketball court.

How about the teacher with a keen radar, sensing the student who is on the margins, the one who's battling depression, the one who isn't getting attention at home, or who is struggling to read. She assigns interesting books that encourage, excite, and give hope to her students. She creates reports and presentations setting her students up to succeed if they'll put forth the effort, despite their learning challenges and family lives. She gets them on the hot lunch program or free counseling appointments when she senses a need. She acknowledges those whom no one else seems to see. Challenges those who are bored. Makes all of her students feel important and valued. She shines her light. In a classroom.

Or the barista who knows all of her customers by name and their usual orders. She asks about their kids, days, plans for the weekend. She makes each customer leave with not only a hot, bold cup of dark roast or a frothy, spicy chai, but also with a smile, the gift of being known, that somebody cares. She's shining her light. In a coffee shop.

Jesus never said we had to be the same kinds of lights, He just said we had to let them shine. What kind of light did He create you to be? What gifts were you given by grace? How are you using them?

Let it shine. Let it shine. Let it shine.

Are you shining your light? Because if we're meant to bring out "the God-colors" in this world, I want to light it up like a spectacular prism!

Jesus continues in the book of Matthew: "If I make you light-bearers, you don't think I'm going to hide you under a bucket, do you? I'm putting you on a light stand. Now that I've put you there on a hilltop, on a light stand—shine!" (Matthew 5:16 MSG).

Are you hiding your light under a bucket?

I love the part in the hymn when the lyrics say, *Hide it under a bushel . . .*

And then the kids, lined up in their Sunday best, shout emphatically, *No!*

Because, no way on my watch am I going to hide this light inside of me.

But in real life, away from the church and school auditoriums and risers, sometimes we're reluctant, hesitant, or afraid to shine our lights. Because our lights might feel different or weird or because someone might not like our light or accept it. But Jesus tells us to go stand on a hill, on the top of a light stand to shine our lights.

Where has God put you? In what circles? With what people? In what circumstances? How can you let your light shine there?

Let it shine. Let it shine. Let it shine.

In 2017, white supremacists gathered in Charlottesville, Virginia. Reverend Osagyefo Sekou had trained a group of folks to be a calming force—a counterprotest to the group rooted in hate. Sekou describes the supremacists cursing and yelling, and the crowd gathered that day feeling unsettled and tense. He had a plan A, a silent counterprotest, but instead he instinctively broke into "This Little Light of Mine."[2]

A grown man stood in front of a heated, hostile group of people who claimed superiority based on their skin color. He planned on leading others to stand with their lips sealed but then broke into this children's song. He stood on his "hill," and he let his light shine. And people joined in. Because that's how light works. It's contagious.

Sekou said that the supremacists "didn't know what to do with all that joy. We weren't going to let the darkness have the last word."[3]

Because light brightens the darkness every single time.

We sang another song around the evening campfires at Marmon Valley Horse Camp while roasting bread on sticks for dinner. Yes, we actually took bread dough, stretched it out on a stick and cooked it over a fire. I don't remember the word for it, but I do remember how delicious the soft, earthy bread tasted warm from the flames.

The lyrics from "Pass It On" went so well with the smoky air, since it only takes a spark of light to start a figurative fire of God's love.[4] A pop song from a few years back that hit number six on the *Billboard* Hot 100, "Fight Song,"[5] has the same message. Rachel Platten sings about how it only takes the light of a single match to create an explosion.

That's what this minister did. Took his little spark and touched the candle next to him, and the one next to that, until a joyful noise filled the air, and the anger and tension of a protesting crowd were overwhelmed by the flames of light and dissipated.

There is darkness in the world. Hate. Anger. Prejudice. Fear. Lust. Greed.

But we are lights. Commissioned and empowered by Jesus.

One version of this hymn says, *Don't let Satan blow it out.* (Are you picturing kids with bangs and crooked collars blowing on their fingers as if they were birthday candles on a cake? I am.)

I'm gonna let it shine.

We need to hold on to this mantra. To let our lights shine, even in the dark spaces, especially in the dark places. Because our single matches and sparks light up a room, a heart, a family. Our little lights chase out the darkness and replace it with God-colors—vibrant, inviting, peaceful, and filled with love. Our unique glow, our distinct gifting when illuminated, brightens the places we go and the people we encounter. And then those spaces are filled with light for others to experience and share.

And those people are all lit up. They, in turn, spread the powerful positive light of Christ wherever they go next, to whomever they next meet.

So what kind of light do you have? And how are you going to let it shine?

Let it shine. Let it shine. Let it shine.

CONTEMPLATE

You're here to be light, bringing out the God-colors in the world. God is not a secret to be kept. We're going public with this, as public as a city on a hill. If I make you light-bearers, you don't think I'm going to hide you under a bucket, do you? I'm putting you on a light stand. Now that I've put you there on a hilltop, on a light stand—shine! (Matthew 5:14–16 MSG)

1. When reading this chapter, what light has God reminded you about that He's sparked in your heart?

2. How do you plan on letting your little light shine this week?

28

IN THE GARDEN

C. Austin Miles, 1912

I come to the garden alone
While the dew is still on the roses;
And the voice I hear falling on my ear
The Son of God discloses.

And He walks with me, and He talks with me,
And He tells me I am His own;
And the joy we share as we tarry there,
None other has ever known.

He speaks, and the sound of His voice
Is so sweet the birds hush their singing;
And the melody that He gave to me
Within my heart is ringing.

I'd stay in the garden with Him
Though the night around me be falling,
But He bids me go; through the voice of woe
His voice to me is calling.

How Hymns Remind Us We're Not Alone

I am a horrible gardener. I'm trying to think of the last thing I planted that actually grew, and I'm drawing a blank. The bell peppers my son and I tried to grow in the bed at the side of our driveway last summer—shriveled. The wildflowers I intently planted on the grave of our beloved pet tortoise so our kids could find beauty there, so we wouldn't lose sight of where Howard rests—I thought they sprouted, but those turned out to be weeds. Where did the wildflower seeds go?

And yet, no matter how bad I am at it, throughout my life I keep finding myself in gardens.

Which actually makes sense, because God more or less began everything in a garden.

> Now the LORD God had planted a garden in the east, in Eden; and there he put the man he had formed. The LORD God made all kinds of trees grow out of the ground—trees that were pleasing to the eye and good for food. (Genesis 2:8–9)

In fact some of my earliest memories are of pulling weeds in the hot July sun, the earthy scent of tomato plants and soil cocooning me, sweat dripping and stinging the corners of my eyes, in the garden plot my mom and her friend Muriel rented each summer. They split the small fee to farm a 20' x 20' parcel of land—more space than either of our yards could provide for planting. The young mamas tilled and fertilized the soil. They devoted three mornings a week to nurturing their tomatoes, beans, peas, and zucchini. I look back at them in awe, working the land, creating fresh produce long before "farm fresh" was chic. They couldn't leave us kiddos home alone, so they dragged us along, assigning us simple tasks to keep us occupied. Plus, we were allowed to eat fresh sugar snap peas from the vine—crisp and sweet and tasting like summer air. Our weeding and watering also gave us purpose, like we were contributing to all of this miraculous growth of food from the ground.

How fitting. The first task God gave mankind was to tend to the garden.

> The LORD God took the man and put him in the Garden of Eden to work it and take care of it. (Genesis 2:15)

The summer between my junior and senior year of college I studied at Regent's University London. Just ten minutes from my dorm the sweet perfume of roses overtook me as I strolled through Queen Mary's Rose Garden, lush with some 12,000 fragrant, delicate blooms.[1] This was a completely new kind of garden for me—intentionally engineered and designed for the sole purpose of beauty. I'd never experienced anything as spectacular and abundant—gorgeous beds of fragile, pale pink roses planted across beds of lemon-yellow flowers flanking beds of rounder, flatter blooms with a thick, drippy smell, like honey. The excess was extravagant. In the midst of an intense course load and my first time in a foreign land, I found comfort and peace among the blossoms.

I wasn't familiar with the hymn "In the Garden" at that time, but listening to it now, I feel like C. Austin Miles saw my twenty-one-year-old self and penned these words for the coed alone in England, who was invigorated by the adventure, but struggling to convert dollars to pounds, maneuver the Tube, and figure out what to eat for breakfast in the dining hall, because smelt on toast and baked beans in the morning turned my stomach.

I come to the garden alone, while the dew is still on the roses, and the voice I hear falling on my ear, the Son of God discloses. And He walks with me, and He talks with me . . .

Jesus was with me in London. Walking with me. Talking with me. Making sure I wasn't alone. Just as He's with us each step of our lives.

Fast-forward more than twenty years. My youngest has this passion for planting. Even after the failed pepper experiment last summer, he's full-on committed to trying again this year. We went to the local nursery and purchased pots of tomatoes and a lush basil plant. Tiny radish sprouts are already peeking their green leaves out of the almost-black dirt where he planted their seeds in our yard, along with long, stringy green tops of garlic. I'm not a gardener, but God keeps bringing me back to gardens.

Is that just me?

I don't think so. Is there a garden in your memory? One you currently tend or explore or go to for solace and solitude? These natural sanctuaries bring us back to

God's creation, back to the pivotal places in Jesus's plan to rescue us from our sin, sadness, and struggles.

On the night of His betrayal, Jesus went to the Garden of Gethsemane—not a pumpkin patch or formal flower garden, but an olive grove—to talk with God. They went back and forth, wrangling through the toughest of situations. They worked through it together, and Jesus prayed God's will would be done (Mark 14; Matthew 26; Luke 22). God's will was that Jesus would suffer and die on the cross, be our sacrificial lamb, that His blood would clear mankind's sins, replace the Jewish law, and make us righteous and whole for eternity. Not because God wanted to punish His Son, but because God wanted to save each and every one of us. Jesus did too. They loved us. They still do. This is what the Father and Son chatted about in a garden.

That was on Thursday night. Sunday morning, the resurrected Jesus appeared to Mary Magdalene in another garden. In fact, at first she thought Jesus was the *gardener* (John 20:11–17). Mary was devastated. Her beloved teacher, friend, advisor, and advocate had been brutally tortured and killed. She thought He was the Messiah. Her heart was shattered. But then she saw Him. Whole. Breathing. Radiant. Mary touched Jesus, alive, not defeated by death, but victorious. And her broken heart must have instantly mended and felt like it would burst again, but this time with joy.

C. Austin Miles wrote "In the Garden" apparently not for my study abroad moments, but as an expression of a vision he saw while studying Mary's encounter with Jesus in John 20.[2]

He speaks, and the sound of His voice, is so sweet the birds hush their singing, and the melody that he gave to me, within my heart is ringing.

Yet, the lyrics of this hymn reach us all in our own personal gardens. In our beginnings, in our work, in our wrestling, in our joy, Jesus walks beside us. He wants to talk with us.

And He walks with me and He talks with me, and He tells me I am His own.

How incredible that this is His desire! Makes me want to seek out a garden pronto. To feel the wind tousling my hair, inhale the richer, earthy scents of outdoors like tilled soil and grass clippings, hear frogs chirruping in a pond or the buzz of a bee flitting from flower to flower, maybe even see my breath on a cold, winter morning reminding me to be grateful for the very air I breathe.

Because this is what I need every day. How about you? A daily walk and talk with our Savior. His sweet voice a melody hushing out the noise of the world, bringing us joy and peace, reminding us He'd do anything for us; in fact, He already did. Telling us again and again that we are His, His beloved sons and daughters.

CONTEMPLATE

He asked her, "Woman, why are you crying? Who is it you are looking for?"

Thinking he was the gardener, she said, "Sir, if you have carried him away, tell me where you have put him, and I will get him."

Jesus said to her, "Mary."

She turned toward him and cried out in Aramaic, "Rabboni!" (which means "Teacher"). (John 20:15–16)

1. What is your favorite place to walk and talk with Jesus?

2. Is there a garden nearby—a rock garden, a public formal garden, a greenhouse, an art gallery with paintings of gardens, a vegetable garden where you can go? Commit to finding a garden, any kind, this week and to spending half an hour walking and talking with Jesus there. You could bring your Bible, a journal, your earbuds and favorite worship music, or stroll in silence. You choose how you feel you'll best connect with Him.

29

JOYFUL, JOYFUL, WE ADORE THEE

Henry Van Dyke, 1907

Joyful, joyful, we adore thee,
God of glory, Lord of love;
Hearts unfold like flowers before thee,
Opening to the sun above.
Melt the clouds of sin and sadness;
Drive the dark of doubt away;
Giver of immortal gladness,
Fill us with the light of day!

All thy works with joy surround thee,
Earth and heaven reflect thy rays,
Stars and angels sing around thee,
Center of unbroken praise.
Field and forest, vale and mountain,
Flowery meadow, flashing sea,
Singing bird and flowing fountain
Call us to rejoice in Thee.

Thou art giving and forgiving,
Ever blessing, ever blessed,
Wellspring of the joy of living,
Ocean depth of happy rest!
Thou our Father, Christ our brother,
All who live in love are thine;
Teach us how to love each other,
Lift us to the joy divine.

Mortals, join the happy chorus,
Which the morning stars began;
Father-love is reigning o'er us,
Brother-love binds man to man.
Ever singing, march we onward,
Victors in the midst of strife,
Joyful music leads us sunward
In the triumph song of life.

How Hymns Bring Us Joy

The decision to play softball was a disaster.

I roamed around dusty left field with the leather glove my dad had conditioned with a musky-smelling oil stretched wide open, arm extended as high as I could into the air, eyes up—hoping against hope to catch a glimpse of the white ball against the blue sky and somehow position myself underneath it to catch it.

I rarely did. Three eye surgeries and no depth perception for this star player of the Astros in her caution-tape yellow jersey made judging the height and distance of the round leather ball as it rocketed into the air nearly impossible.

No matter how hard I chased it, that ball didn't want to be caught.

What do you want to catch?

A fly ball? A husband? A break? The bad guy? A firefly? Definitely not the measles or the flu. How about joy?

Christian author, speaker, and podcaster Annie F. Downs says, "Joy will not chase you, but it loves to be caught."[1]

Sigh. Unlike that softball, joy loves to be caught.

In 1907, Henry Van Dyke took the final movement of Beethoven's Ninth Symphony, added lyrics, and created a hymn proclaiming where to find joy[2]—because if it likes to be caught, we should start chasing it, right? I mean, who doesn't want more joy in their life?

"Joyful, Joyful, We Adore Thee" reminds us in the midst of traffic jams, leaky faucets, disappointments, and anxiety that we can still find joy—the same joy even the stars recognize, the joy of knowing no matter who we are, how we "measure up," how we're feeling about ourselves today, God, the King of the universe, the Holiest, the Creator of it all, that God? He loves us.

Mortals, join the happy chorus, which the morning stars began; Father-love is reigning o'er us.

Inhale that truth. Exhale. Inhale it again.

God's love is reigning over you!

But it's hard sometimes, isn't it? When you get turned down for the grant or the award, when your team loses, when the inspector finds termites, when the storm keeps the people you love from visiting. How do you find joy?

By seeking God.

When we seek Him, when we tell God all about the hurt and shame and frustration. When we ask for His help, guidance, or comfort. When we chase the joy He offers, it can be found. This hymn even gives us the words to sing or pray, a way to ask, to help us find joy again, Dear God:

Melt the clouds of sin and sadness; drive the dark of doubt away; Giver of immortal gladness, fill us with the light of day!

The Bible declares this joy is ours. That joy will overtake us, that joy is our strength, that joy will fill us!

Those the LORD has rescued will return.
They will enter Zion with singing;
    everlasting joy will crown their heads.
Gladness and joy will overtake them,
    and sorrow and sighing will flee away.

(Isaiah 35:10)

The joy of the LORD is your strength. (Nehemiah 8:10)

Though you have not seen him, you love him; and even though you do not see him now, you believe in him and are filled with an inexpressible and glorious joy, for you are receiving the end result of your faith, the salvation of your souls. (1 Peter 1:8–9)

Peter, the fisherman whom Jesus told, "Follow me"; the same guy who pretended he didn't know Jesus when

Jesus was arrested by the Jewish religious leaders; the same Peter who used to be called Simon, but Jesus redefined him by changing his name to "The Rock" (way before Dwayne Johnson was born); that same Peter said if we believe in Jesus, then we are filled with inexpressible and glorious joy. It's there. Just waiting to be caught. But we need to make sure our gloves are open. How?

By returning to the blessings God showers on us. Because God's love and blessings are everywhere.

Last night we had the wrong address to my daughter's soccer game. After three U-turns, *yikes*, I ended up getting her and her teammate to their pregame warm-up thirty minutes late. They were jittery. I was stressed. The only reason I avoided hitting another car while backing into a parking spot was that they blared their horn just in time. The girls raced out of the car, which needs a wash and an oil change, and I took a deep breath.

Before checking my phone, or sprinting out of the car after them, I paused. I thanked God for getting us there safely, for keeping me from having an accident in the parking lot, for arriving before the game began, for a gorgeous, sunny spring evening. All blessings. All gifts. My tension began to dissolve.

With twenty minutes until game time, I thanked God for the hour He'd provided me in the kitchen (between one child's previous activity and time to leave for this game), and for my sweet twelve-year-old who wanted to cook with me there. I praised God for food on the fly and ate the warm, zesty homemade mac 'n' cheese we'd pulled out of the oven just in time to scoop in a plastic container. I felt satisfied, grateful.

Out of my car in time for the whistle, I caught a whiff of fireworks. It's only May, with the grind of the last two weeks of school to trudge through, but for a minute it smelled like summer, like bare feet in the warm grass, Fourth of July and family gathered under the stars, freedom. I went from tense to joyful.

I couldn't undo getting lost or being late. I couldn't wave a magic wand and have our whole family gathered together at the dinner table. I couldn't redo my parking fiasco. But I could chase joy, put out my glove, and be filled with it.

All Thy works with joy surround Thee, earth and heaven reflect Thy rays, stars and angels sing around Thee, center of unbroken praise.

Yes, life can be chaotic, and sometimes filled with turmoil. But God is bigger, brighter, bolder, better than all of it. I want to catch His joy, even in the midst of awkward, tense, and painful moments and seasons. I want to raise my hands high, open my glove as wide as it will go, ready to catch the inexpressible joy Jesus offers. It's going to be overflowing.

Will you join me?

Ever singing, march we onward, victors in the midst of strife; joyful music leads us sunward in the triumph song of life.

I think we're going to need some giant-sized gloves.

CONTEMPLATE

Though you have not seen him, you love him; and even though you do not see him now, you believe in him and are filled with an inexpressible and glorious joy, for you are receiving the end result of your faith, the salvation of your souls. (1 Peter 1:8–9)

1. Go on a treasure hunt today to catch some joy with your glove. Find one thing you *see* that brings you joy, one thing you *touch* that brings you joy, one thing you *smell* that brings you joy, one thing you *hear* that brings you joy, and one thing you *taste* that brings you joy.

2. Repeat every day this week.

30

AMAZING GRACE

John Newton, 1779
Last verse: author unknown, before 1800

Amazing grace! How sweet the sound
That saved a wretch like me!
I once was lost, but now am found;
Was blind, but now I see.

'Twas grace that taught my heart to fear,
And grace my fears relieved;
How precious did that grace appear
The hour I first believed!

Through many dangers, toils and snares,
I have already come;
'Tis grace hath brought me safe thus far,
And grace will lead me home.

The Lord has promised good to me,
His Word my hope secures;
He will my shield and portion be,
As long as life endures.

Yea, when this flesh and heart shall fail,
And mortal life shall cease,
I shall possess, within the veil,
A life of joy and peace.

The earth shall soon dissolve like snow,
The sun forbear to shine;
But God, who called me here below,
Will be forever mine.

When we've been there ten thousand years,
Bright shining as the sun,
We've no less days to sing God's praise
Than when we'd first begun.

How Hymns Transform Us

In the Broadway musical *School of Rock*, shy Tomika barely says a word for the first act of the show. Then one day in class (in act 2) out of nowhere she belts out:

Amazing grace! How sweet the sound that saved a wretch like me . . .

The entire cast freezes as her voice pierces the air. Time stops. How everyone perceives Tomika shifts with that one song. She goes from being the girl who must not have any talent—otherwise she surely would have auditioned for the band—to being the girl with the unbelievable voice that needs to be showcased front and center. Tomika's own opinion of herself changes too. She shifts from being uncertain and doubting her abilities to confident in her gifting.

This is the power of "Amazing Grace." It takes us from being one thing, to being something unbelievably better, totally other than what we were. From lost to found. From blind to being able to see.

The first time I cried during the hymn "Amazing Grace" was at my grandma's funeral twenty-one years ago. Yes, I was sad about losing my grandma. She was the only grandparent I ever really knew. Grandma played paper dolls with me. She listened to my stories as if they mattered and was one of the most genuinely kind people I've ever met. But she was sick. Emphysema destroyed her lungs after decades of smoking. Inhaling and exhaling air was so much work, I believe she was ready to let go of her earthly body and trade it for a heavenly new one that could breathe effortlessly.

I was there the day she died. Although she was unconscious, when I told Grandma how much I loved her, she stirred and made a sound, which must have been so difficult for her to muster. I know she heard me. She understood.

So, yes, I cried for the passing of my grandma at her funeral, but that's not what undid me when I sang "Amazing Grace."

There was something different about the Laura who showed up to Grandma's funeral than the one who had last stood in this small chapel next to the church I grew up in. My grandmother, Mary Margaret Wheeler, whom everyone called Peg, had gotten a fresh new pair of lungs and the freedom to breathe heavenly air. Me? I'd been given a fresh soul, and I was free to breathe in my freedom in Christ.

I'd last been in the historic brick building with wooden pews surrounded by stained glass windows during my college years. The chapel was used only for smaller gatherings, but from time to time growing up I'd peek in the white, front double doors, just to inhale the scent of something older—the oiled wood floor and the yellowing pages of the hymnals. I'd gaze at the soft sunlight, watercolored and subdued through the glass.

Back then I'd been living a dual life, reading my Bible before bed, then tucking it under my pillow in the apartment I shared with three sorority sisters. It was comforting that Jesus loved me, but I didn't live like I believed it, didn't apply what His love meant. I was on the high-speed train to proving myself, all by myself, no matter what the cost.

I pushed myself academically, enlisted in student organizations, traveled abroad, anything to gussy up my résumé, and prove to anyone, including myself that maybe, just maybe I was worth something. I did the same thing with guys, but that was uglier. Doing almost anything to get their attention, then trying to keep it. Of course when the relationships or crushes or whatever you want to call them ended, I felt worthless all over again.

That was me back then. Always striving. Never feeling like I'd achieved enough, done enough, was pretty or funny or smart enough to make anyone truly like me on any playing field. Never believing there was anything I could ever do to earn love, respect, or worthiness. Basically, a complete wretch.

But at Grandma's funeral, I had a job, and the amazing man who married me stood by my side. Somebody thought I was capable and hardworking enough to hire. More importantly someone decided I was loveable enough to marry. I still couldn't believe it.

Most importantly, I'd gone from habitually reading a couple of familiar Bible verses, as if by rote, and then shoving them somewhere no one, not even I, could see, to seeking Jesus again. My husband was a big part of that, but that's a story for another time. Now, as a young woman in my midtwenties, I began to understand that the Bible wasn't just a "quick fix" when I was sad or afraid, but it was the living Word of God. It was my road map for how to live. As I took more time for God, He reminded me over and over again, "You are loved. You are redeemed. You are forgiven. You are a treasure. You are enough."

Enough? Me?

I'd always been told I had to do more, be more, achieve more. That I would never be enough. And I believed every word. Now God whispered daily that I *was* enough.

And then this song.

I once was lost, but now am found; was blind, but now I see.

It seemed to speak everything God and I had been talking about over the last two years all at once. It summed up who I had been the last time I was in this chapel, and who I was now, who I'd always been, but just hadn't believed it, had been too blind to see it.

I think I've cried every time I've heard "Amazing Grace" since that day. It doesn't matter what version—the classic hymn on an organ, the contemporary hit with a new bridge describing how Jesus breaks our chains by Chris Tomlin,[1] Hillsong's new take on it, "Broken Vessels."[2] They all undo me. Play it on the bagpipes, and I'm a goner.

Through many dangers, toils and snares, I have already come. 'Tis grace hath brought me safe thus far, and grace will lead me home.

It feels like God literally wrapping His arms around me, looking me in the eye and saying, "You once were lost, but I found you. You've been through many toils and snares, gotten tangled up in so many places you shouldn't have been, had your eyes closed, blinded to the glorious living I planned for you. Open them now. See how much I love you. Let my amazing grace soak over you."

And today as God again speaks these words to my heart, my face is soaked with tears of gratitude. Because, how sweet the sound of His words.

Are you trying to do more? Be more? Achieve more? God speaks these words to you too.

Jesus spoke this grace over a man who was born blind, who because of his disability had no place in his society. Jesus showed that man he had value, he mattered. Jesus healed him.

His neighbors and those who had formerly seen him begging asked, "Isn't this the same man who used to sit and beg?" Some claimed that he was.

Others said, "No, he only looks like him."

But he himself [the blind man] insisted, "I am the man."

"How then were your eyes opened?" they asked.

He replied, "The man they call Jesus made some mud and put it on my eyes. He told me to go to Siloam and wash. So I went and washed, and then I could see." (John 9:8–11)

Was blind but now he sees. Was once a beggar, but now walking around transformed so completely people didn't even recognize him. This is what Jesus's amazing grace does. Changes everything.

Jesus spoke this grace to Saul, a man passionate about killing Christians. In Acts 9, Jesus knocks Saul over, temporarily blinds him, and asks, "Saul! Saul! Why are you persecuting me?" (v. 4 NLT).

It changed everything.

Jesus shook up Saul and told him he wasn't supposed to be exterminating followers of Jesus, but instead should be using his passionate personality to spread the gospel—the good news that Jesus loves and saves us. Saul listened. Jesus gave Saul back his sight, not just to see the physical world, but to see spiritually how loved he was by Jesus. Saul changed his name to Paul, representing that his heart had changed, and went from trying to squash the church, to being possibly the greatest evangelist of all time. He went from being one thing, to something completely different.

God spoke these healing assurances to the former British slave trader John Newton, who wrote the hymn, "Amazing Grace," in the late 1700s.[3] God's grace-filled words must have sounded something like this: "John, you used to be a hateful trader of human beings, but now you're mine. Now you're whole, complete, and loved." Newton did a one-eighty and became an abolitionist and Anglican clergyman. God speaks these same words to you. *You are whole. You are complete. You are loved.*

It's just a song, right?

Not for me.

Not for Tomika or Newton or hundreds of others who have sung "Amazing Grace" and realized that because of what Jesus did for them, the muck, the yuck are gone, forever. We've been set free. And this is the glorious truth of the gospel. We are sinners. We mess up. Every. Single. Day. But Jesus loves us so much that He died for us, showering us with grace. We don't have to do anything to receive it. It's free and ours for the taking. That's what is so amazing about it! And now our hope is secured for *as long as life endures.*

Because of Jesus, anyone who believes in Him has gone from one thing to something unbelievably, amazingly better.

I once was lost, but now am found; was blind, but now I see.

How sweet is that sound?

CONTEMPLATE

"How then were your eyes opened?" they asked.

He replied, "The man they call Jesus made some mud and put it on my eyes. He told me to go to Siloam and wash. So I went and washed, and then I could see." (John 9:10–11)

1. How has Jesus opened your eyes? What do you see differently, the more you hang out with Jesus?

2. Knowing that Jesus died for you, that His grace is amazingly free, how does that change you? What were you before? What can you be now?

3. Thank Jesus for the sweet sound of His grace in a prayer—you can write it out here, in your journal, or say it in your head.

Afterword

COME SPOTIFY
WITH ME!

You might have figured out by now that I love music. We dive into thirty hymns in this book but reference many more songs. I've created three playlists on Spotify to share with you some of the music that inspires me. You can find them under my Spotify profile (laurasmithauthor) or search for these playlists:

1. *How Sweet the Sound: Favorite Hymns from the Book* (spotify:playlist:1EJgjlxmfvRtJunAWIXcc7). This playlist consists of my favorite versions of fifteen of the hymns in this book.

2. *How Sweet the Sound: Old and New Mix* (spotify:playlist:6aYG2dZkyBghqXHYQU23N1). This is a fun playlist—a mix of some of my favorite worship songs that have roots and potentially even lyrics straight from traditional hymns.

3. *How Sweet the Sound: Worship on Repeat* (spotify:playlist:5oKZrrCcAnF86yXriw4YXv).

The songs on this list are considered contemporary worship music, not hymns, but they are so powerful to me and point me back to Jesus over and over again.

I hope you enjoy!

ACKNOWLEDGMENTS

Maddie, your pure love and kindness is a beautiful melody to this world.

Max, the music you make both literally and figuratively is a joyful noise unto the Lord.

Mallory, your joy spreads like a gorgeous chorus everywhere you go.

Maguire, your creative spirit is music to the Master Creator's ears.

I love you all beyond words. My M&M's, you are the most beautiful music to my soul.

Mom, thank you for holding the hymnal up for me before I could do it on my own and for teaching me from an early age that, yes, Jesus loves me.

Bob Hostetler, I am blessed beyond measure to have your wise, kind, faithful self in my corner as my agent. Thank you for sending the email that set this in motion with the subject line, "Hymns?"

Amy Parker, thank you for letting me borrow your family hymnal for inspiration while writing this book. But much more, thank you for listening, guiding, igniting, laughing, crying, and walking this writer's journey with me from the first page of my first book and every word since.

Beth Troy, I am so grateful for you as a "writer friend," but even more for the ways you help me understand Jesus on a deeper level. Each time we're together, I discover a new facet of Him and His love.

Tammy Bundy, my writing twin and musical advisor —thank you for cheering me on, being willing to look at my words (and make them better), and mostly for your invaluable friendship.

Shena Ashcraft, your passion and energy for books, words, and Jesus is contagious. Thanks for feeding my creative fire and walking alongside me in my faith.

To my editor, Dawn Anderson, thank you for taking on this project and seeing it through to the finish. I am forever grateful for your expertise and time.

To everyone on the Our Daily Bread Publishing team, including John van der Veen, Melissa Wade, Emily Van Houten, Anna Haggard, Cathy Sall, Rochelle Traub, John Boggs, Mary Hauschild, and countless others, thank you for all your support in every last detail. You've taken my musings on the power of hymns and turned them into a beautiful book.

Mike Nappa, thank you for having the vision for this book and inviting me into it. Thank you for helping me hone my craft. I am a better writer because of you.

NOTES

CHAPTER 1

1. James D. Smith III, "Where Did We Get the Doxology?," *Christian History* 31 (1991), accessed March 26, 2019, https://christianhistoryinstitute.org/magazine/article/where-did-we-get-the-doxology.

2. Quoted in Ryan Romeo, *OUTCRY* (Franklin, TN: Worthy Publishing 2016), xiv.

CHAPTER 3

1. Library of Congress, "African American Spirituals," Library of Congress Celebrates the Songs of America (collection), accessed November 15, 2017, https://www.loc.gov/item/ihas.200197495/.

2. Sarah H. Bradford, *Harriet, The Moses of Her People* (New York: Lockwood & Son, 1886). Reprint, Chapel Hill, NC: University of North Carolina at Chapel Hill Library, 2012. Available online at https://docsouth.unc.edu/neh/harriet/harriet.html.

CHAPTER 4

1. Italicized quotations roughly follow Psalm 96 (ESV) as recited by Andi Rozier of Vertical Church Band, now Vertical Worship, *Church Songs*, Essential Worship, 2015.

2. Hymnary.org search results, accessed November 2, 2018, https://hymnary.org/search?qu=scripture%3Apsalm%2096%20 in%3Atext.

3. Kathy Svitil, "Deciphering Mystery Bee Flight," CalTech, November 29, 2005, accessed February 25, 2019, https://www .caltech.edu/about/news/deciphering-mystery-bee-flight-1075.

CHAPTER 5

1. "Come, Thou Fount of Every Blessing," Hymnary.org, accessed March 2, 2019, https://hymnary.org/text/come_thou_fount_of _every_blessing.

2. The Bundys, "Come Thou Fount of Every Blessing," *Louisiana Avenue*, 2015.

CHAPTER 6

1. Ph.D., "Story behind the Song: It Is Well with My Soul," *The St. Augustine Record*, October 16, 2014, sec. Lifestyle, https://www.staugustine.com/article/20141016/LIFESTYLE /310169936.

2. Kristene DiMarco, "It Is Well," *You Make Me Brave*, Bethel Music, 2014.

CHAPTER 7

1. Hillsong Live, "Cornerstone," *Cornerstone*, Hillsong, Capitol, Sparrow, 2012.

2. Josh Baldwin, "Stand in Your Love," *Victory*, Bethel Music, 2018, https://www.essentialworship.com/songs/stand-your-love.

3. Vertical Worship, "The Rock Won't Move," *The Rock Won't Move*, Provident Label Group, 2013.

4. "My Hope Is Built on Nothing Less," Hymnary.org, accessed March 14, 2019, https://hymnary.org/text/my_hope_is_built _on_nothing_less.

CHAPTER 8

1. C. Michael Hawn, "History of Hymns: 'I Love to Tell the Story,'" Discipleship Ministries, The United Methodist Church, June 27, 2013, https://www.umcdiscipleship.org/resources /history-of-hymns-i-love-to-tell-the-story.

2. "I Love to Tell the Story," Hymnary.org, accessed March 19, 2019, https://hymnary.org/text/i_love_to_tell_the_story_of _unseen_thing.

3. For more insights on this Scripture: Timothy J. Keller, "Sharing the Joy We Have in Christ" (sermon, Redeemer Presbyterian Church, New York, NY, January 17, 2019), https://gospelinlife .com/downloads/sharing-the-joy-we-have-in-christ/.

4. Annie F. Downs, *100 Days to Brave* (Grand Rapids: Zondervan, 2017), 5.

CHAPTER 9

1. "Frances Havergal Wrote 'Take My Life and Let It Be,'" Christianity.com, April 28, 2010, https://www.christianity.com /church/church-history/timeline/1801-1900/frances-havergal -wrote-take-my-life-and-let-it-be-11630571.html.

CHAPTER 10

1. C. S. Lewis, *The Screwtape Letters* (London: Bles, 1942).

2. "Be Thou My Vision," Hymnary.org, accessed February 13, 2019, https://hymnary.org/text/be_thou_my_vision_o_lord _of_my_heart.

CHAPTER 11

1. Nicholas Sparks, *The Last Song* (New York: Grand Central Publishing, 2010), 118.

2. Passion, Kristian Stanfill, "Jesus Paid It All," *Everything Glorious*, Sparrow/sixsteps, 2006.

CHAPTER 12

1. "What a Friend We Have in Jesus," Hymnary.org, accessed April 2, 2019, https://hymnary.org/text/what_a_friend_we _have_in_jesus_all_our_s.

CHAPTER 13

1. Def Leppard, "Rock of Ages," *Pyromania*, Bludgeon Riffola Limited, 1983.

2. "Rock of Ages, Cleft for Me," Hymnary.org, accessed April 16, 2019, https://hymnary.org/text/rock_of_ages_cleft_for _me_let_me_hide.

3. Ben E. King, "Stand by Me," *Don't Play That Song!*, Atco, 1961.

CHAPTER 14

1. Richard W. Adams, "Turn Your Eyes Upon Jesus," Cyber Hymnal, last modified December 11, 2019, http://www .hymntime.com/tch/htm/t/u/r/turnyour.htm.

CHAPTER 15

1. Lee Strobel, *The Case for Christ: A Journalist's Personal Investigation of the Evidence for Jesus* (1998; repr., Grand Rapids: Zondervan, 2013).

2. Mosaic MSC, "Tremble," *Unknown*, Provident Label Group, 2017.

CHAPTER 16

1. Ira Sankey, *My Life and the Story of the Gospel Hymns* (New York: Harper & Brothers, 1906), 333, quoted in Richard W. Adams, "Nothing but the Blood," Cyber Hymnal, last modified December 9, 2019, http://www.hymntime.com/tch/htm/n/b/t /nbtblood.htm.

CHAPTER 17

1. "Three in One," Library of Juggling, http://libraryofjuggling .com/Tricks/3balltricks/ThreeInOne.html.

2. Dr. Seuss, *The Lorax* (New York: Random House Children's Books, 1971), 49.

3. Search results for "3-in-1" on QVC website, accessed April 23, 2019, https://www.qvc.com/catalog/search.html?keyword= 3-in-1.

4. Melanie Greenberg, "Americans Just Broke a New Record for Stress and Anxiety," *Psychology Today*, February 19, 2017, https://www.psychologytoday.com/us/blog/the-mindful-self -express/201702/americans-just-broke-new-record-stress-and -anxiety.

5. Holy, Holy, Holy," Hymnary.org, accessed May 1, 2019, https:// hymnary.org/text/holy_holy_holy_lord_god_almighty_early.

6. Phillips, Craig, and Dean, "Revelation Song," *Fearless*, INO, 2006.

CHAPTER 19

1. "Obituary of Obie Edwin Philpot," Tributes.com, November 7, 2013, http://www.tributes.com/obituary/show /Obie-Edwin-Philpot-96640742.

2. He's Got the Whole World in His Hands," Hymnary.org, accessed May 7, 2019, https://hymnary.org/text/hes_got_the _whole_world_in_his_hands.

3. Bob Goff, *Everybody Always: Becoming Love in a World Full of Setbacks and Difficult People* (Nashville: Nelson Books, 2018), 5.

CHAPTER 21

1. Chris Brown (@chrisdotbrown), Instagram.

2. Eric Wyse, "The History Behind the 'Old Rugged Cross,'" Lifeway Christian Resources, September 22, 2015, https://www.lifeway.com/en/articles/the-history-behind-the-old-rugged-cross-hymn-george-bennard-revival.

CHAPTER 22

1. Silent Night, Holy Night," Hymnary.org, https://hymnary.org/text/silent_night_holy_night_all_is_calm_all; "Stille Nacht," Hymnary.org, https://hymnary.org/tune/stille_nacht_gruber; and Richard W. Adams, "Silent Night," Cyber Hymnal, last modified December 7, 2019, hymntime.com/tch/htm/s/i/l/silnight.htm.

2. "Silver Bells," composed by Jay Livingston and Ray Evans, 1950.

3. Jane Austen, *Mansfield Park*, ed. Tony Tanner (1814; repr., Middlesex, England: Penguin Books, 1975), 283–84.

4. "Silent Night," Carols.org.uk, https://www.carols.org.uk/silent_night.htm; "Notes" in "Silent Night, Holy Night," Hymnary.org, https://hymnary.org/text/silent_night_holy_night_all_is_calm_all.

CHAPTER 23

1. "He Will Hold Me Fast," Cyber Hymnal, last modified December 10, 2019, http://www.hymntime.com/tch/htm/h/w/i/hwilhold.htm.

2. Enneagram Two ("The Helper") with a One-Wing ("Servant") refers to my basic personality type. For more on this and other personality types, see the Enneagram Institute, https://www.enneagraminstitute.com/type-descriptions.

CHAPTER 25

1. Hillsong United, "Whole Heart (Hold Me Now)," *People*, Hillsong, 2019.

2. "John Wesley Work" (person page), Hymnary.org, accessed May 7, 2019, https://hymnary.org/person/Work_JohnWesley 1873.

3. John Wesley Work Jr., comp., *Folk Songs of the American Negro*, ed. Frederick Jerome Work, 2 vols. (Nashville: Work Bros. & Hart, 1907). GodTube Staff, "Go Tell It on the Mountain," GodTube.com, accessed May 7, 2019, https://www.godtube.com/popular-hymns/go-tell-it-on-the-mountain/.

CHAPTER 26

1. GodTube staff, "Tis So Sweet to Trust in Jesus," GodTube.com, available March 20, 2019, https://www.godtube.com/popular-hymns/tis-so-sweet-to-trust-in-jesus/.

CHAPTER 27

1. This song was later adapted by Zilphia Horton in connection with the civil rights movement.

2. Eric Deggans, with contributions to digital version by Daoud Tyler-Ameen, "'This Little Light of Mine' Shines On, A Timeless Tool of Resistance," *All Things Considered*, American Anthem, NPR.org, August 6, 2018, https://www.npr.org/2018/08/06/630051651/american-anthem-this-little-light-of-mine-resistance.

3. Osagyefo Sekou quoted in Deggans, "'This Little Light of Mine' Shines On."

4. Kurt Kaiser, "Pass It On," *Kurt Kaiser: Pass It On*, Word, 1972.

5. Rachael Platten, "Fight Song," *Wildfire*, Columbia Records, 2015. Lyrics available at https://www.azlyrics.com/lyrics/rachelplatten/fightsong.html.

CHAPTER 28

1. Queen Mary's Gardens, The Royal Parks, accessed May 13, 2019, https://www.royalparks.org.uk/parks/the-regents-park /things-to-see-and-do/gardens-and-landscapes/queen-marys -gardens.

2. GodTube staff, "In the Garden," GodTube.com, accessed May 15, 2019, https://www.godtube.com/popular-hymns /in-the-garden/.

CHAPTER 29

1. Canopy Social, "Chase Joy—A Message from Annie F. Downs," Canopy / North Point Ministries, January 30, 2019, https://canopysocial.com/blog/chase%20joy.

2. "Joyful, Joyful, We Adore Thee," Hymnary.org, accessed May 16, 2019, https://hymnary.org/text/joyful_joyful_we _adore_thee.

CHAPTER 30

1. Chris Tomlin, "Amazing Grace (My Chains Are Gone)," *See the Morning*, Sparrow/sixsteps, 2006.

2. Hillsong Worship, "Broken Vessels (Amazing Grace)," *No Other Name*, Capitol, Hillsong, Sparrow, 2014.

3. "Amazing grace! (how sweet the sound)," Hymnary.org, https:// hymnary.org/text/amazing_grace_how_sweet_the_sound.

ABOUT THE AUTHOR

Best-selling author and speaker **Laura L. Smith** is a music lover. She grew up singing old hymns in her traditional church, then rushing home to count down the rest of the Top 40 on *Billboard*'s music charts with Casey Kasem. Smith loves all kinds of music but typically listens to worship music. And although she can't carry a tune, she's often seen singing or dancing around her house. Smith speaks around the country sharing the love of Christ with women at conferences and events. She lives in the college town of Oxford, Ohio, with her husband and four kids. Find out more at www.laurasmithauthor.com.

Help us get the word out!

Our Daily Bread Publishing exists to feed the soul with the Word of God.

If you appreciated this book, please let others know.

- Pick up another copy to give as a gift.
- Share a link to the book or mention it on social media.
- Write a review on your blog, on a bookseller's website, or at our own site (ourdailybreadpublishing.org).
- Recommend this book for your church, book club, or small group.

Connect with us:

- @ourdailybread
- @ourdailybread
- @ourdailybread

Our Daily Bread Publishing
PO Box 3566
Grand Rapids, Michigan 49501 USA

✉ books@odb.org